Early praise for *Forge Your Future with Open Source*

This book has needed to exist for a long time. Newcomers to free and open source software now have a thorough guide to participation, and the author's real-world experience shows on every page. Among the book's strengths is that it not only explains what steps to take (and their variants), but also shows new contributors how things look from the project's point of view. I hope and expect to see this book referred to by contributors to projects across the internet.

➤ **Karl Fogel**
   Partner, Open Tech Strategies, LLC

If you ever wished you could have a compendium of HOWTO open source from one of the most knowledgeable folks in this biz, this is the book for you. Vicky is an absolute gem and has successfully distilled decades of knowledge into an easy-to-access format that should be required reading for anyone wanting to get into FOSS.

➤ **Katie McLaughlin**
   Director, Django Software Foundation, Python Software Foundation

The next time someone tells me they want to learn more about open source, I'll have the perfect book recommendation. Vicky has written the concise, practical guidebook we were missing. *Forge Your Future with Open Source* is an excellent quick-start guide for anyone stepping into the world of open source.

➤ **Rikki Endsley**
   Community Manager, Opensource.com, Red Hat

Wonderfully readable, not only as a practical manual, but as an engaging and inspirational introduction to the world of free software, one practical and people-oriented example at a time. This is the book I wish I had read many years ago.

➤ **Chris Lamb**
  Debian Project Leader

I've been working in open source for almost two decades. I went to Microsoft a decade ago to open-source .NET and C#. I wish I'd had a copy of VM's book. This book offers valuable historical context and practical guidelines on how and when to work on an Open Source project. *Forge Your Future with Open Source* will no doubt empower the next generation of contributors and I'm envious of their bright futures!

➤ **Scott Hanselman**
  Program Partner Manager, Open Source .NET, Microsoft

Vicky's book is the "Goldilocks" guide to participating in open source: just the right information, with neither too much obscure detail nor too little actionable advice. I look forward to recommending it to others.

➤ **Cat Allman**
  Board Member, USENIX

Contributing to a free software project is one of the best ways to help the free software movement, and this book is the comprehensive, self-contained guide you need to get started. Brasseur skillfully balances depth and breadth, homing in on key points around the mechanics of contributing as well as the oft-neglected meta areas of effective communication, licensing, and employment ramifications.

➤ **John Sullivan**
  Debian Developer

Forge Your Future with Open Source goes where no book has gone before, clearly teaching how to get started as a contributor to open source, explaining why contributing is valuable and rewarding, and exploring the technical and social challenges both new and experienced contributors face, in an honest and practical way.

➤ **Allison Randal**
  Board Member, Open Source Initiative

In her inimitable style, VM Brasseur brings a useful cheat sheet for contributing to free and open source software. There is probably something in this book for everyone to learn.

➤ **Karen Sandler**
  Co-Organizer, Outreachy

Vicky unflaggingly reminds us that creating software is a liberal art—and the foundational art of Open Source is courtesy. If every reader were to practice some of the advice in this book, the software world would be a more welcoming place.

➤ **Robert "r0ml" Lefkowitz**
  Distinguished Engineer, ACM

Open Source runs most of the technology world, from mobile phones to the internet. Despite it being open, there are many hidden rules in how teams work together. Vicky's glorious book removes the arcane barriers surrounding this field and takes us along a journey into Open Source from the practice, the culture, the community, the history, the motivation, and even how we talk to each other. It is a book built on years of practice that not only needed to be written but deserves to be read by anyone wanting to contribute to this field.

➤ **Simon Wardley**
  Researcher, Leading Edge Forum

Forge Your Future with Open Source

Build Your Skills. Build Your Network.
Build the Future of Technology.

VM (Vicky) Brasseur

The Pragmatic Bookshelf

Raleigh, North Carolina

Our Pragmatic books, screencasts, and audio books can help you and your team create better software and have more fun. Visit us at *https://pragprog.com*.

The team that produced this book includes:

Publisher: Andy Hunt
VP of Operations: Janet Furlow
Managing Editor: Brian MacDonald
Copy Editor: Paula Robertson
Indexing: Potomac Indexing, LLC
Layout: Gilson Graphics

For sales, volume licensing, and support, please contact *support@pragprog.com*.

For international rights, please contact *rights@pragprog.com*.

ISBN-13: 978-1-68050-301-2
Book version: P1.0—October 2018

Contents

Preface

Here we are—forty years on from the launch of the Free Software movement and twenty years since the "open source" and its related movement were created—and it's still really hard to contribute to most free and open source software projects. There are all of these unspoken rules, unfamiliar language, and a lack of documentation that would be impressive were it not so unfortunate. The web is full of articles about how to contribute, but none of them cover everything you need to make your first contribution. You end up playing contribution Whac-a-Mole,[1] with a new problem or unspoken rule popping up the moment you think you know what's going on. It's all so frustrating sometimes.

Don't Panic, I'm here to help. Welcome, my friends, to the book that finally makes sense of contributing to open source.

What's in This Book?

In these pages, you'll find everything you need to start contributing to free and open source projects. First, we'll cover the history and philosophies of these movements, since without that knowledge, you'll trip and fall on the very first step of your journey to becoming a contributor. After that, we'll investigate the benefits of contributing to free and open source and help you select a project that suits your needs, so both you and the project can benefit from your contribution. Obviously we'll cover how to make the contribution itself, but we'll also discuss the many ways you can contribute without writing a line of code. All of those unspoken rules will be revealed, and we'll even talk about how to start your own open source project.

What's NOT in This Book?

This book will not hand you a list of free and open source projects where you should start contributing. Not only would such a list be out of date the moment

---

1. https://en.wikipedia.org/wiki/Whac-A-Mole#Colloquial_usage

it was published, but it also wouldn't be the right list for everyone. Thousands of free and open source software (FOSS) projects exist in the world today. It would be silly to list a few, then send all of you stampeding off to contribute to just those. With so many projects to choose from, you can find a project that matches your specific skills and interests. In fact, there's an entire chapter to help you do just that.

This book also does not recommend which tools to use for contributing. The most effective tool is the one that works for you (as long as the end product meets the requirements of the project).

I've gone to great lengths to try not to influence your choice of project or tools, while giving you the information and support you need to make your own decisions. You do you, honey.

Who Should Read This Book?

From experienced software professional to new student, anyone who wishes to contribute to FOSS will find value in this book. While most people think FOSS contributions are only the realm of programmers, nothing could be further from the truth. Software development is a multidisciplinary undertaking. Writers, testers, designers, project managers, marketers… There's a place for everyone in free and open source software.

While this book contains some technical concepts, it does not assume that you are a programmer, that your contribution will be code, or even that you're overly familiar with software development. Free and open source software needs all sorts of contributions, submitted by all sorts of people.

Why Is This Book Not Openly Licensed?

Yeah, I thought someone might ask that.

With the growing awareness and importance of open source along with the explosion of new projects released every year, it's more important than ever that there be a resource to enable and support the immense number of new contributors we're going to need to help maintain that software. This book is that resource.

While this book needed to exist, and I was well equipped and well placed to write it, it wasn't going to happen if I did it on my own. Without external help or motivation, I know that I would never finish a project this huge. I mean: writing a book? That's really intimidating.

To make this happen, I needed help. Enter Pragmatic Bookshelf. Their experience and support could guide and motivate me to create this book, but only if they administer the copyright of it. This allows them to do things like negotiate translations and similar administrative duties, with which I have no experience whatsoever.

The choices were:

1. I assign copyright of the book to Pragmatic, then have their invaluable support to help bring it into the world, and Pragmatic chooses a book license based on their current business practices.

2. I retain copyright, but I do it alone and unsupported, so the book is never started, finished, nor released under any license at all.

This book is an important resource that is long overdue and will help thousands of people and free and open source software projects. That it finally exists is more important to me than my copyright. So I chose Option 1. I have no regrets. Pragmatic are great people.

Suggestions, Errata, or Questions?

Free and open source software is all about the community coming together to collaborate and build something amazing. This book is no different. Do you have suggestions for how to improve the book for future generations of contributors? Problems with the content? Share your thoughts using the errata submission form on the book's catalog page on the Pragmatic Bookshelf website.[2]

Also, if you have any questions at all about contributing to free and open source software, join us on the #fossforge channel on the Freenode Internet Relay Chat (IRC) network. A web interface[3] is available to make joining easy, as well as a quickstart guide[4] if you're not familiar with IRC. The channel community will gladly help support you in your journey from novice to contributor.

Credits

I mostly wrote this book on a 2016 MacBook Pro, in Markdown, using MacVim as my text editor and git as my version control, though more than a few pages were written on a 9.7" iPad Pro using the Textastic text editor and

---

2. https://pragprog.com/titles/vbopens/errata
3. https://webchat.freenode.net/?channels=%23fossforge
4. https://opensource.com/life/16/6/irc-quickstart-guide

WorkingCopy git client. The diagrams are my creation, using OmniGraffle. The font in the diagrams is *Open Sans*, created by Steve Matteson and licensed under the Apache 2.0 open source license. The handwriting font used in several examples is *Nothing You Could Do*, created by Kimberly Geswein and licensed under the Open Font License. The Kannadan font used in *When It Goes Wrong* is *Kedage* by the Indian Language Technology Solutions Project and is licensed under the GNU General Public License version 2.

Acknowledgments

Books don't happen easily, and they don't happen solely through the force of will of their authors. True to the spirit of free and open source software, a lot of people contributed to the creation of this work.

To every free and open source community member and leader who was patient and generous with their guidance and advice over the years and who helped me learn what was necessary for this book: Thank you.

To the Opensource.com community moderators, whose brilliance and insight never fail to inspire me to be a better human and contributor: Thank you.

To the technical reviewers, and particularly to those who gave up part of their 2017 holiday to review the first half of the book: Thank you. The reviewers were (in alphabetical order by first name): Alessandro Bahgat, Andrea Goulet, Ashish Bhatia, Ben Cotton, Daivid Morgan, Derek Graham, Donna Benjamin, Emanuele Origgi, Fabrizio Cucci, Glen Messenger, John Strobel, Johnny Hopkins, Karen Sandler, Karl Fogel, Katie McLaughlin, Máirín Duffy, Maricris Nonato, Mark Goody, Matthew Oldham, Michael Hunter, Mitchell Volk, Nick McGinness, Nouran Mhmoud, Peter Hampton, Raymond Machira, Rikki Endsley, Robin Muilwijk, Scott Ford, Stephen Jacobs, Tibor Simic, and Zulfikar Dharmawan. If any errors or omissions still exist in the book, the fault is entirely mine for ignoring their advice.

To Chethan R Nayak, for providing the Kannadan translation used in *When It Goes Wrong*: Thank you.

To Sage Sharp, for wisely suggesting I add a section to *Prepare to Contribute* about roles commonly found in FOSS projects: Thank you.

To Ben, John, Katie, and Rikki, for their invaluable counsel during the title selection process: Thank you.

To the Pragmatic team, for believing this book was a good idea and providing a happy and supportive home for it: Thank you.

To Brian, my editor and my friend, who came to me with a crazy idea and who helped me turn it into reality, without whom I *literally* could not have done this (pun intended): Thank you.

To everyone on the channel, who knows who they are and who are there for me through it all: Thank you. I love each and every one of you and I will never tire of saying so.

And finally to you, who will help shape the future of technology through your free and open source contributions: Thank you.

CHAPTER 1

The Foundations and Philosophies of Free and Open Source

When we think or talk about free and open source software, there's a strong tendency to focus on that last bit: the software. Software, as we all know, is just made out of code, right? So isn't free and open source software, therefore, all about the code? It's all programming, but it's programming that anyone can use, like, for FREE, man. After all, that's what the *free* means in "free and open source", right? You can use it, but there's no cost. Yup, that's open source. Book done. We can all move along.

You've probably already guessed that the previous paragraph was a steaming pile of misinformation. Unfortunately, it's based on a lot of the common misconceptions about free and open source software. These fallacies are repeated and perpetuated to the point of being seen as common knowledge. As is often the case with things like this, not everything that is common qualifies as knowledge.

It's About the People

For instance, despite what many believe, free and open source software is not only about the *software*; it's also about the *people*. People build the software, employing varied skills like writing, testing, designing, and (yes) programming. People maintain the software and form tight-knit communities to support both the software and its users. It was through the vital and deep-seated convictions of people that free and open source software exists at all. Those convictions form the basis of a philosophy of freedom and sharing that enabled the world-changing idea, "software should be Free," to evolve into the massive social movement that we today know as open source.

To participate in free and open source software, it's critical that you understand that, while it's tightly entwined with software and technology, it is fundamentally a social movement. Social movements are composed of people, and as we know, people are difficult, squishy, amazing things. Contributing to free and open source is not simply a mechanical process of pushing code from here to there. To contribute, you must understand the underlying social constructs and philosophies that are common to all free and open source software projects.

Why Learn About the Philosophies?

"But!" you interject, "I'm not here to learn about philosophy and stuff. I just want to contribute! Why tell me all this?"

Without these philosophies, there would be no free and open source software. While it may not always be obvious, the freedoms and beliefs of the founders of the free and open source movements underpin everything in each project you use and contribute to. The participants in most free and open source projects are aware of these philosophies and will expect you to be, as well. The few minutes you spend reading this chapter will provide valuable context that allows you to better understand the motivations behind many of the actions you'll see taken in open source projects.

It could be that after learning the basic philosophies, you find you're either drawn to or repelled by them. This is an important realization to have at this point. It will guide you toward those projects that best suit your own beliefs, away from those that don't, or perhaps away from contributing at all. If that's the path you choose: Congratulations! Few people are self aware enough up front to avoid devoting so much of their free time to a pursuit that doesn't appeal to them. The time you spend learning and thinking about these philosophies now can save you days, weeks, months, or more in the future.

Free and Open Source Software Is Everywhere

Free and open source software is everywhere. Your car, TV, and even your light bulbs probably run software using the *Linux* kernel and related operating system. Your phone either runs on an open source platform—*Android*—or it has a proprietary platform but runs apps written in an open source language—*Swift*. The movies you watch may have been created using the *Blender* free and open 3D rendering suite, and they certainly were converted or edited with the help of *ffmpeg*, a free software tool for manipulating digital media files. You may open your open source browser—*Firefox*—to watch a live stream delivered by the free *Open Broadcaster Software*. You may then place an order from an online merchant, who built their website using the free and open *Wordpress*, *Drupal*, or *Joomla*. Thanks to the *OpenSSL* cryptographic library and tools, you know that your financial information will remain secure.

Free and open source software (*FOSS*) has become the default choice for programming languages, infrastructure, databases, content management systems, and web servers among many other categories of technology. There are millions of free and open source projects, performing billions of different tasks. Every year GitHub, an online service for hosting and developing software and a major supporter of open source, releases a report of the GitHub and open source world. It calls this study *The Octoverse*. The 2017 Octoverse report[1] shows more than 25 million open repositories on GitHub alone, and this number is just a fraction of the open projects available.

As mentioned earlier, free and open source is more than just software: it's people. Each project is built by people for people. People use, contribute to, and support the projects. And people form organizations dedicated to cultivating and advancing the free and open source software movements. These organizations exist all over the world, in nearly every region. In the USA, you can support the Free Software Foundation,[2] the Software Freedom Conservancy,[3] the Open Source Initiative,[4] or Software in the Public Interest,[5] among others. In Europe, you have Free Software Foundation Europe,[6] Open Source Projects EU OSP),[7] and Open Forum Europe (OFE). Australasia is supported by Linux Australia,[8] Opensource.asia,[9] and FOSSAsia.[10] Groups like Free and Open Source Software For Africa (FOSSFA)[11] and OpenAfrica[12] support, teach, and spread free and open source technologies across many countries in Africa. Central and South America are also highly active in the free and open source world, thanks

1.   https://octoverse.github.com
2.   https://www.fsf.org
3.   https://sfconservancy.org
4.   https://opensource.org/
5.   https://www.spi-inc.org
6.   https://fsfe.org/index.en.html
7.   https://opensourceprojects.eu
8.   https://linux.org.au
9.   http://opensource.asia
10.   https://fossasia.org
11.   http://www.fossfa.net
12.   https://africaopendata.org

to groups like Software Livre Brasil,[13] FLISOL,[14] and Grup de Usuarios de Software Libre Perú[15] among dozens of others.

Other Open Movements

The open ethos isn't limited to software. A number of related movements have sprung up in the past few decades, each dedicated to sharing, transparency, and collaboration.

Wikipedia[16] is the most well-known and highly trafficked of these open movements. Anyone in the world is encouraged to contribute to its ever-growing knowledge base. The majority of the content on Wikipedia is available under a license furnished and maintained by Creative Commons.[17] Creative Commons is an organization that promotes the free sharing and reuse of creative works like music, writing, art, and data by providing copyright licenses that can be applied to them. This standard and well-understood body of licenses helps people share their works while still protecting their valuable copyright.

Wikipedia and Creative Commons are far from the only non-software open movements. Open Knowledge International[18] empowers society through open data. Internet Archive[19] aims to provide free and open access to all the world's knowledge. Open access academic journals ensure the free and open flow of fundamental research. The Open Source Seed Initiative[20] maintains open access to plant genetic resources that might otherwise be locked behind patents. These are just a few of the many ways that the free and open ethos has permeated our culture.

This philosophy of open access and sharing goes back thousands of years, but how did it become so prevalent in software?

---

13. https://softwarelivre.org
14. https://flisol.info
15. https://www.softwarelibre.org.pe
16. https://wikipedia.org
17. https://creativecommons.org
18. https://okfn.org/about/
19. https://archive.org
20. https://osseeds.org

The Origins of Free Software

Before you start to contribute to free and open source software projects or join their communities, you should probably know something about the nature and philosophies of FOSS and how it got where it is today.

In the early days of computers, all software was free to acquire, use, inspect, modify, and share. Researchers, computer operators, and computer hardware manufacturers all gladly distributed their software works to others. At the time, the profits were in the hardware sold, not in the software that ran on it. No one had yet considered that software could be a revenue stream, largely because each model of hardware was highly specialized, such that the software written for one model would not run on another. A single piece of software could not be widely used, so there was no profit from selling it. If the software enabled the sale of more of the highly profitable hardware, then computer manufacturers were thrilled that people would share that software with each other. It was exactly like today– when you might buy a game console because it's the only platform with the game you want to play–but with mainframes instead of gameframes.

All good things come to an end. Eventually manufacturers recognized not only the value the software provided to users but also the amount of effort that went into developing it. Where there's value there's profit, so these companies started software development as its own industry distinct from the creation of the computer hardware on which it ran. As the profits began to roll in for the software developers, some operators—who were used to using and sharing software—started to resent not only the new cost of acquiring software but also that they could no longer modify it for their needs and then share the updated software with others.

In 1983 Richard M. Stallman (RMS),[21] frustrated that software operators were no longer free to inspect, modify, and share software, announced the launch of the GNU Project.[22] This project is dedicated to the creation of a UNIX-compatible operating system built of components that are entirely free to use, modify, and distribute. Two years later, the GNU Manifesto[23] followed. It declared the fundamental beliefs of the project and launched Free Software as a movement.

---

21. https://en.wikipedia.org/wiki/Richard_Stallman
22. https://en.wikipedia.org/wiki/GNU_Project
23. https://en.wikipedia.org/wiki/GNU_Manifesto

The Four Freedoms are the core of the free software movement. Those freedoms—which in standard programming fashion, are numbered starting from zero—are:

0. The freedom to run the software however you wish and for whatever reason you wish.

1. The freedom to study the software source code and make whatever changes you wish.

2. The freedom to copy and distribute the software (modified or not) however you wish.

3. The freedom to make improvements to the software and then share the improved version however you wish.

Any software that does not guarantee these freedoms to its users cannot be considered "free" because it limits the users' rights in some way. To help guarantee these rights and freedoms, RMS, the GNU Project, and the newly formed Free Software Foundation (FSF)[24] created software licenses that leverage the pre-existing concepts of copyright. The FSF *copyleft* licenses (a play on the word *copyright*) provide more than just the permission to use software released under them; they ensure that software can never violate the Four Freedoms. While many people believe that the Four Freedoms are Stallman's greatest invention, in fact his most far-reaching and brilliant contribution to software is the recognition that copyright can be used in this way, and that careful copyright licensing can enforce software freedom. This invention paved the way for the open source movement that followed.

The Origins of Open Source

The free software movement grew in popularity and awareness throughout the 1980s and 1990s and attracted the attention of business interests. The release of the Netscape web browser as free software in 1998 amplified this attention. While businesses were intrigued by the potential of open software development, many were less thrilled with the strong political, philosophical, and activist nature of the free software movement and its supporters.

In early 1998, soon after the release of the Netscape code, several free software supporters gathered to discuss how the movement might make itself more palatable to business interests, in hopes of increasing the scope, reach, and contributors for open software development. They decided a rebranding was

---

24. https://www.fsf.org

in order and chose the term *open source*—coined by Christine Peterson[25]—as the name for this version of the movement. Many members of the group then created the Open Source Initiative (OSI)[26] as a focal point for their efforts.

One of the first tasks of OSI was codifying what it means to be an open source software project. The Open Source Definition describes the ten responsibilities and requirements a project must fulfill if it wants to qualify as an "open source" project. The OSI has a detailed description of the definition on its website,[27] but the definition can be summarized as:

1. The project must be freely redistributable—even if sold and even if it's part of a larger collection of software.

2. All source code must be available and distributable.

3. Modifications and derived works must be allowed and distributable under the same license terms.

4. If distribution of modified code isn't allowed, it cannot prevent distribution of patch files (snippets of source code that can be applied to include new fixes or functionality) along with the unmodified code.

5. In no way can the license under which the code is distributed discriminate against any person or group. All people must be allowed to use the code on the same terms, even if they're bad people like Nazis.

6. Similarly, the license also can't single out industries, companies, or other types of undertakings. All groups and ventures must be allowed to use the code on the same terms, even if those groups support horrible things (again, like Nazis).

7. The license applies to anyone who receives a copy of the software without needing any additional permissions.

8. The license can't restrict someone from extracting the project or code from a larger collection. If they do extract it, it's available to them under the same license terms as the whole, larger collection.

9. If the software is distributed as part of a larger collection of code, the license can't put any restrictions or requirements on that other code.

10. The license applies to all technology and UI applications of the software to which it's applied.

---

25. https://en.wikipedia.org/wiki/Christine_Peterson
26. https://opensource.org/
27. https://opensource.org/osd

The OSI provides an annotated version[28] of the Open Source Definition. This version is valuable for understanding the meaning and importance of the definition. It details rationales and supporting information for each of the criteria for a project to qualify as "open source."

Most of these criteria apply to the *license* under which a project is distributed. To aid people in selecting a license that meets all of the criteria, OSI reviews licenses and maintains a list of OSI-approved open source licenses.[29] If a project claims to be "open source" but is not released under an OSI-approved license, then the project cannot call itself "open source."

This focus on license is a critical part of free and open source software. It's the license and its directives that make a piece of software open source, not merely the availability of the source code. Without the application of an OSI-approved license, code can be at best "source available" but not open. The legal mandates contained in the license ensure that the code is available and that people are free to do with it what they wish (within the constraints of the license). Code and projects that do not have license files, even if they have been bequeathed to the public domain, are not open source.

Difference Between Free Software and Open Source

One question that everyone asks when they first discover FOSS: "What's the difference between Free and Open Source?" This is a surprisingly contentious question, but a very good one to ask. From a code and project perspective, there's very little effective difference between the two. Most of the licenses that the FSF considers "Free" are also OSI-approved, and many of the OSI-approved licenses support the Four Freedoms and therefore, are also considered "Free" by the FSF. There are some outliers on each side, but there is far more similarity than difference between the two families of licenses. In most cases, Free Software is also Open Source. In slightly fewer cases, Open Source is also Free Software.

The difference between Free and Open Source comes down to one of philosophy and motivation. For supporters of Free Software, the effort has a strong moral purpose. Just as all people should be free from oppression and abuse, all software should be free from any restrictions of use, reuse, and distribution. To do otherwise is to limit the potential of the software and the people who use it. This is the driving force behind the Free Software movement: Freedom.

---

28. https://opensource.org/osd-annotated
29. https://opensource.org/licenses

Open Source, on the other hand, finds its motivation in what it deems more practical matters. To supporters of open source, business, science, art, and all other endeavors that employ software are better served if the source for that software is publicly available. To them, it's simply logical that opening the source enables types and levels of innovation that would be impossible with proprietary (closed source) software. This logic appears to be supported by the explosion of open source-based software companies and services in the nearly twenty years since the advent of "open source" as a movement.

To dramatically oversimplify it: Free software sees software freedom as a moral matter; open source sees it as a practical one. This is not, however, a hard and fast rule, nor is it a matter of two separate and disagreeing factions. The "difference" between free and open source software is actually a spectrum of a single belief that humanity is better served when software is freely and openly available. Supporters of free and open source software all fall somewhere on that single spectrum, but they all believe that freely and openly available software is a very good idea indeed.

From the perspective that matters most for this book—the nuts and bolts of contributing to a project—there is virtually no difference between free and open source software. Looking solely at contribution processes, there's usually no way to tell whether a project is free software or open source until you look at the LICENSE file.

An Aside About Terminology

As you participate in free and open source software projects, you'll find that people sometimes are a bit sensitive about the terminology used to refer to their movement of choice. While from a contribution point of view, there isn't much effective difference between free or open source projects, from a philosophical point of view, there is. The Freedoms guaranteed by free software form a fundamental belief system for many free software advocates. Therefore, some of them become sensitive to free software projects being referred to as "open source." To them, doing so dilutes the emphasis on Freedom embodied in the movement and removes the opportunity to teach new people about the freedoms and their moral importance. Regardless of your personal opinion, respect the Free Software movement and do not call free software projects "open source."

Also, you'll often see Free Software referred to as Free/Libre Software. This stems from the ambiguity of the word "free" in the English language. To those who are unfamiliar with the philosophy that underlies the movement, "free" may mean purely "free of charge" or "gratis." Because it's unlikely these people paid for the software, it's perfectly reasonable for them to think that there's no deeper meaning behind the word. "Libre," on the other hand, is not burdened with the multiple meanings that "free" carries. Stemming from "liber," the Latin word for "free" (as in freedom), Libre in modern languages is unambiguous in its meaning...for those who know its meaning, that is. Whether using "free" or "libre," the free software movement must educate those who use it in the underlying philosophy of the software they use, contribute to, and perhaps distribute.

Whichever type of project you join—free/libre or open—take note of how it prefers to be labeled and respect that choice.

Because the contributing process is similar for both free and open source projects (inasmuch as there is similarity between projects at all), and because I support both the free and the open source philosophies, in this book I use "free," "open source," and "FOSS" ("free and open source" abbreviated) interchangeably with a preference for "free and open source." I don't use "free/libre and open source" or "F/LOSS", because I find these terms clumsy, and after the introduction to free and open source above, entirely unnecessary. There is no ambiguity when "FOSS" is used in this book, so there's no need for "F/LOSS."

A Brief Introduction to Copyright and Licensing

A lot of the content above has been all "license" this and "license" that without a lot of context on what a license actually is and why it's such a big deal, particularly for free and open source software.

So it's time for a very brief introduction to copyright, a complicated matter without which free and open source software wouldn't exist. As you saw above, Richard Stallman realized that he could use the existing copyright laws and systems to ensure software would always remain Free through careful licensing. Copyright therefore underpins everything in FOSS. Without it, and without an understanding of it, FOSS is not possible. Keep in mind: copyright law is a complex subject, so this is only a rudimentary introduction. Also, I am not a lawyer. What follows is not legal advice, only guidance to help you understand some of the basic concepts and complications of copyright.

When you create something, be it artwork, music, writing, software code, or any other creative endeavor, by default you own the copyright over that thing. This is an oversimplification, because in some countries and jurisdictions, you have to register something to get copyright. It's not as common anymore, but it's common enough that you might want to check on how copyright is assigned in your country.

However the assignment happens, as the copyright owner, you have the right to control how that thing can be used. This control comes through *licensing* the work. A license is a legal document used to give people or entities permission to use copyrighted material. If someone else would like to use your work in any way, you can provide them a license that details the specific ways they may use your creation. A creator can apply the statement "All Rights Reserved" to their work to indicate that they don't want anyone to reuse or repurpose their work in any way; the creator has reserved the reuse or repurposing rights for themselves alone.

Things become complicated when there are multiple creators of a work. Each one of the creators, by default, retains copyright over the portions that they contributed to the whole work. If you program a piece of software, you have copyright over the code you wrote for it. If I come along and add a unit test for your software, I have copyright over the code I wrote for that test. The entire piece of software now has two copyright holders involved somehow.

Free and open source software licenses can help when there are multiple copyright holders for a single piece of software. These licenses often (but not always) contain a statement requiring contributions to a project (the unit test in the above example) to be contributed and released under the same license as the original work. This helps to keep the copyright and licensing complexities more comprehensible. As you can imagine, in a large project, questions of copyright could easily become mind-bendingly complicated.

Whatever creative work you contribute to a project, unless you agree to assign your copyright elsewhere (as can happen in a work for hire or a Contributor License Agreement situation, both covered later in the book), you retain copyright over your contribution and—if the project is released under an OSI-Approved License—your contributions will be publicly available. This means you can build a professional portfolio without fear of breaking copyright law or violating someone else's copyright.

This is not the case for creative work you contribute for your employer. Internships, freelance, hourly, and full-time jobs are all what is called *work for hire*. Unlike FOSS contributions, by default, the copyright on any work you contribute to a work for hire situation *belongs to the organization paying you*. Once you contribute that work to the organization, you no longer have any rights over it at all, and you *may not share it* in any form without very express and very written permission. It is *illegal* to share any creative work for which you do not have copyright or that is not licensed in such a way that it may be made public. This holds true for code, designs, documentation, project plans, or anything else that you create in a work-for-hire situation.

If you are interviewing or applying for a new position, and the prospective employer asks for work samples, you *must not* share anything that you created for past or current employers unless you can demonstrate that they have given you permission to do so. If you share private and proprietary work of past employers, how do you think that makes you look to your potential employers? Answer: Like a thief. You will have just proven to them that you cannot be trusted to keep their secrets. Why would they want to hire someone like that?

A portfolio comprising contributions to free and open source software contributions avoids the legal, moral, and reputational risks of sharing samples from proprietary work-for-hire creations. It not only allows you to highlight your skills, but it also demonstrates that you are ambitious and passionate enough about technology that you're willing to dedicate time outside of work to learn and contribute back to the community.

Because nothing is simple where copyright law is involved, there are, of course, exceptions to the work-for-hire copyright ownership rule. This comes in the form of employment agreements, proprietary information assignment agreements, and similarly named and intentioned legal documents. These usually come into play when you start employment with an organization, and they detail who owns the intellectual property (has the copyright) for what creations in which situations. Often these will declare that anything created on company property (computers) and/or on company time is the property of the company. However, thanks to the rise of free and open source software, some companies such as GitLab[30] and GitHub[31] have employment agreements that allow employees to retain copyright over their free and open source software contributions for the duration of their employment, regardless of when or how these contributions were created. This practice isn't yet common, and you should carefully read and review your employment agreements before signing them, regardless.

On the other side of the copyright ownership exception coin, we have Contributor License Agreements (CLA). These are discussed further in Chapter 3. Some (but not all) CLAs include the requirement that the contributor assign the copyright of all of their project contributions to the organization that

---

30. https://about.gitlab.com/2017/12/18/balanced-piaa/

31. https://github.com/blog/2337-work-life-balance-in-employee-intellectual-property-agreements

oversees the project. This gives the organization the ability to enforce that copyright, or even to change the license under which the project is distributed, without having to bother every contributor to ask their permission. CLAs are legal documents, and like all legal documents, it's important that you read them before you sign so you know what you're getting yourself into.

Types of Free and Open Source Software Licenses

The best place to learn about the various types of free and open source software licenses is the Open Source Initiative Licenses list.[32] It can be a little overwhelming at first, so to get you started, here's a quick introduction to the two basic types of FOSS licenses: copyleft and permissive.

Per the Open Source Definition, mentioned in *The Origins of Open Source*, both types of licenses share the requirement that anyone who uses works licensed under one of them must be able to view, modify, and share the source of the work. The difference comes after that: What can the user then do with the work? Can they change the terms under which people can use it? Or must the work be redistributed under the same terms by which the user received the original work?

For software distributed under a *permissive license*, someone who makes a change and redistributes the software is *permitted* to change the terms and conditions under which someone can use the new distribution (also known as a *derivative work*). In other words, the creator may change the license of the derivative work to one that's different from the original work. This affords the person releasing the new distribution a lot of flexibility in defining how the derivative work may be used. Permissive licenses also allow a creator to use a work released under this type of license in a proprietary work. When that proprietary work is released, it can remain proprietary. The permissive license of its component(s) does not force the creator to release the work under any sort of free or open source license. Two popular permissive licenses are the Apache License[33] and the MIT License.[34]

While permissive licenses allow a creator a lot of flexibility when distributing a derivative work, copyleft—or reciprocal—licenses protect a work from being relicensed under what may end up being a more restrictive set of terms and conditions. Once a work has been released under a copyleft license, the license ensures that the work can never be released under a license that may in any

---

32. https://opensource.org/licenses
33. https://opensource.org/licenses/Apache-2.0
34. https://opensource.org/licenses/MIT

way remove or diminish any of the original rights and freedoms (specifically, the Four Freedoms mentioned in *The Origins of Free Software*) granted to the user by the license. A redistributed or derivative work released under a copyleft license must also not add new restrictions to what the user may do with the work. This ensures that this work, once freed, will forever be free. Copyleft licenses also have a requirement that any derivative works made from software licensed under one of them and distributed must be released under the same terms and conditions as the copyleft-licensed work. This is the *reciprocal* nature of this type of license: if your creation benefits from a copyleft licensed work, then anyone who receives your creation must similarly benefit from your work. The GNU General Public License (GPL)[35] is the most common copyleft license. Other copyleft licenses include the GNU Lesser General Public License (LGPL)[36] and the Mozilla Public License.[37]

It probably won't surprise you to hear that, as with every other legal issue discussed in this book, what you've just read is an oversimplification of how these two different types of licenses actually work. Each type contains licenses that are more or less permissive and more or less reciprocal. Generally speaking, of the OSI-approved licenses, the MIT License is considered the most permissive and the GPL one of the most reciprocal. All other licenses fall somewhere along the spectrum between these two.

Now You Have a Strong Foundation

All of this history, philosophy, and law is complicated, I know. Don't feel you have to understand it in depth to contribute to free and open source software. Having the background knowledge of the philosophies, knowing that there are two basic types of licenses and the general characteristics of each type, is more than enough. There are millions of FOSS contributors in the world, and most of them get by very well with no more license knowledge than what you've just learned in this chapter.

Now that you have some sense of what FOSS is and what it's done for the world, you may be wondering what it can do for *you*. The next chapter fills in that blank.

---

35. https://opensource.org/licenses/gpl-license
36. https://opensource.org/licenses/lgpl-license
37. https://opensource.org/licenses/MPL-2.0

CHAPTER 2

What Free and Open Source Can Do for You

The previous chapter explained the history and philosophies behind free and open source software (*FOSS*). For many people, this philosophy is reason enough to contribute, but others need more motivation to devote their free time to participate in FOSS projects. If you're reading this book, you obviously have some interest in contributing, but do you really know what you hope to get out of it? Why would you invest your precious time in something for which you don't get paid?

Contributing to free and open source software doesn't have to be a purely altruistic pursuit. Contributors gain a lot for the effort they invest, and all of those advantages will pay off as their careers evolve.

FOSS Benefits to Your Skillset

Most obviously, contributing to free and open source software allows you to learn and practice new skills in a safe environment. It's possible to learn these skills on the job or in the classroom, but FOSS allows you a larger variety of options not only in skills to learn, but also in opportunities to practice them and gain experience. Sometimes, it may even be a safer place to practice those skills. If you do something wrong on the job, you may be reprimanded or possibly fired. If you do something wrong in class, your grade could suffer. In FOSS, if you do something wrong, you apologize and seek help to learn how to do it better.

This is, of course, an oversimplification of the matter. There still are repercussions for making mistakes when contributing to free and open source software. Thanks to the strongly social aspect of FOSS, sometimes these repercussions can have sustained impact. While you can revert a bad contribution, you can't do the same for hurt feelings. Despite that risk, contributing to free and open source projects is still a relatively safe way to learn new skills that you can apply to your life and your career.

So, what are those skills, anyway?

Communication

Free and open source is composed of people, and therefore, contributing to FOSS projects can do wonders for your communication skills. By necessity, the community around a free and open source project will be distributed, often worldwide. This poses interesting communication challenges for getting anything done in the project. All communication usually is asynchronous due to differences in time zones and maintainer availability. Asynchronous communication often is impersonal communication, which can cause problems. The lack of real-time feedback like body language and facial expressions can lead to misunderstandings and delays. These same problems are common in "real-world" jobs, particularly for distributed teams. You gain experience by contributing to FOSS projects, and this helps you interact better in your day-to-day life and work.

Among the communication skills you can learn by contributing to free and open source is how to ask questions. Blurting out an open-ended and context-free query on the mailing list or issue tracker can lead to a lot of frustration and additional back-and-forth before someone can provide an answer. For instance, "Hey, is anyone else having problems running the latest version on their MacBook?" is a question that can lead to a lot of inefficient back and forth communication as people try to narrow down exactly what sort of a problem you're having. "I'm trying to run the latest version on macOS, but it keeps crashing with a FILE NOT FOUND error. Is this a known issue?" is a much better question and much easier for the community to answer. You've told them the version of the software you're running, the platform you're running it on, the behavior you're seeing, and the error message that accompanies it.

You also can learn how to set up expectations. Will you deliver this feature this weekend, or will it be delayed due to family obligations? Will you be able to complete a task on your own, or will it require the assistance of someone else? This type of communication prevents a lot of disappointment and delay in a project where each person depends on the work of others to proceed with their own.

While this asynchronous communication is necessary for a distributed team of project maintainers, it can lead to an unintentional lack of knowledge of or empathy for the people at the other end of the line. This often ends with someone accidentally saying something that's offensive to others in the group. What is intended as a joke can come across as a personal slight or attack. This is particularly common in diverse communities, with equally diverse cultures and social interaction styles. Paying attention to your words and intentionally practicing your communication styles while contributing to a FOSS project makes you a much more pleasant team member for all of your jobs from there on out.

Finally, the distributed and asynchronous nature of a free and open source project requires that all communication be not only effective but also efficient. You enhance your value to any team by learning things like which types of messages are best suited to which medium: short and ephemeral? use chat; discussion and archived? mailing list; benefit from immediacy? conference call. Knowing how to write a good bug report—one that provides the context, expectations, and actual behavior witnessed—also helps you learn how to write other documents and messages more effectively. Paying attention to how to use your words more effectively and efficiently will make you a more productive communicator overall. The training that contributing to free and open source software provides in how to communicate effectively and efficiently will pay dividends throughout your career. *Interact with the Community* goes into the topic of communication in detail.

Collaboration

If you take courses at a college or university, you undoubtedly have had the experience of doing a group project. You and several of your teammates are partnered up to complete a task. The goal of this is to teach you how to break down a project and collaborate on it with each person sharing the load. The reality usually is that the attempt at collaboration is contrived, and one or two people end up shouldering most of the load for the others.

You'll be happy to hear that this is not what true collaboration is. Free and open source software, due to its inborn distributed nature, requires true collaboration to work well. If there's more than one person involved in the project development, then some sort of collaboration processes emerge. The processes themselves vary from project to project, and they won't always work smoothly, but they typically will be far more effective than those you learned in school. So what are some of these collaboration processes?

For starters, there's the division of labor. Whereas in school you may have been stuck doing the lion's share of the work on an assignment, that's unlikely to happen on a collaborative FOSS project. There are multiple reasons for this. For one thing, as someone starts a task and realizes that it may be larger than they originally thought, in open source they usually start a discussion about the task and how it can be broken up or otherwise staged in smaller parts. This public discussion encourages others to chime in, not only with their thoughts but also with their time to help work on some of those smaller parts. There's no shame in FOSS for saying that a task is too large for one person to tackle alone.

Another reason for dividing the work into smaller pieces is risk management. We'll cover *atomic commits* later on in *Make a Contribution*, but summarized: commiting smaller, discrete pieces of work rather than huge chunks makes the work much easier to review; a small commit has a better chance of receiving a thorough review, and therefore bugs are easier to spot. Atomic commits are also simpler to roll back should something go wrong. Both the review and the easy rollback mitigate the risk of fatal bugs slipping into the project.

Finally, there's the matter of *bus factor*. This is a term you may hear frequently in software development.

> *Bus Factor* is a number equal to the number of team members who, if run over by a bus, would put the project in jeopardy.

A macabre metric, no doubt, but also a helpful one. The worst possible bus factor for a project (or part of a project) is *one*. If only one person is familiar with that piece of the project, and that person goes away, the project will find itself in an uncomfortable position. Therefore, dividing up the labor on a feature or task increases the bus factor for that part of the project. Now, rather than just one person being familiar with that piece of the project, two, three, or more people are. When more than one person is familiar with the work, someone is always there as a backup should one of those people move on for some reason (hopefully on a bus rather than under it).

Tools

Almost as important a lesson as collaboration itself are the tools that make that collaboration possible. While the tools vary from project to project, the general project management, communication, and collaboration ideas those tools represent remain the same both across free and open source projects and even into the private sector. For instance, *issue tracking* not only allows a project to track its bugs and features, but it also helps provide oversight and accountability for the work being performed. If used properly by the addition of copious notes, issue tracking also forms a valuable historical resource that can enable future generations to learn from the experiences of those who came before them.

Without *version control*, real collaboration on free and open source would be nearly impossible. Version-controlled files can be edited by multiple people—sometimes even simultaneously—and then have all of the edits merged into a canonical version of the file. The messages included whenever a change is committed to a version controlled project (*commit messages*) themselves are another valuable historical resource. It's best practice for a commit message to provide details not only of *what is changed* in the commit but also *why* it was necessary and *what problem* the commit fixes. By reviewing a series of good commit messages, it's possible for other contributors to the project to follow its evolution and better determine how to engage with the project and the community around it.

Issue tracking and version control commit messages are two forms of asynchronous communication. Free and open source software collaboration would not function without async communication. The community of contributors for a project may span the globe and certainly will span a variety of personal schedules. Were collaboration to rely purely on real-time communication, no one would ever get anything done. For this reason, many free and open source projects rely heavily on asynchronous discussion methods such as mailing lists. People can read and collaborate on their schedules, and the project can keep moving forward. The ability to express your ideas efficiently in a textual method like a mailing list is a skill that will serve you throughout your career, and few opportunities to learn it will be as practical as participating in a mailing list for a free and open source project.

Best Practices

School is a great place to learn about Big O Notation or the golden ratio, but it's usually not as good for learning about current industry best practices. College graduates entering the workforce often find that while their coursework was heavy on theory, it was relatively light on the practice, technologies, and trends that are required for success on the job. Schools aren't to be faulted in this. They do a great job, but are time constrained in a way that industry is not. Curricula take time to develop, so institutions of higher education often must teach technologies and practices that are at the tail end of current industry usage.

Not so with free and open source software. Because FOSS is constantly moving, evolving, and innovating, many of the current industry best practices either originated in free and open source software development or were perfected by it. Version control, feature branches, unit and integration tests, continuous integration and deployment (CI/CD), design patterns... When you contribute to FOSS, you master many concepts and best practices that you may never get to learn in another environment. More importantly, because you're hands on with these concepts, you have the opportunity to learn not only how they work, but also why they're important to do at all, and learn first hand the difference they make to a successful software project.

Technologies

Despite the fact that it's the very first skill benefit most people consider when they start thinking of contributing to FOSS, new technologies are in fact the least important skill you can learn. Of all of the benefits you can gain by participating in free and open source software development, the technology used by a project—while interesting—may be the benefit with the least staying power across the course of your career.

If you have a career in tech—at a software firm, or working with technology in a different context—your entire career will become a continuous parade of new technologies. Some people are able to build an entire career around a single technology (COBOL, for instance), but the majority of us must constantly be learning The Next Big Thing to stay relevant and employable.

Therefore, the technologies you know and use on a daily basis will be constantly shifting. Not so, all of the other skills mentioned in this section. So once you learn how to collaborate well with a group of distributed and diverse individuals, that's information you'll use for the rest of your life. The people skills you can learn from participating in free and open source software can serve you far better than the technological skills.

That said, you will have plenty of opportunities to learn new technologies with FOSS. Heck, considering how integral free and open source solutions have become to the infrastructure underlying most software and technology today, you may even get the opportunity to help build The Next Big Thing that you would otherwise have to learn from books and blog posts.

FOSS Benefits to Your Career

Many people in technology forget that software isn't the only thing that needs developing; their careers do, too. While your managers and mentors can help here, your career development is your responsibility. It's up to you to make sure you're always learning and moving your career in a direction that makes the best sense for your goals and needs.

Free and open source software can be invaluable here. At work, you learn and use the technologies and architectures that are required for work projects.

These technologies may help pay the bills but may not be what you need to move your career in the direction you want. FOSS, however, offers you endless options for technologies and architectures. Once you determine your goals, you can turn to FOSS to see which projects will help you reach them.

Public Portfolio

Your contributions to free and open source software projects become a public portfolio of your skills and how you've advanced them over the years. As you start contributing to projects, start a log or portfolio for tracking all of your contributions. Don't simply rely on the projects' version control systems and hosting providers, as those can change. If you don't keep your own log of contributions, you can easily lose track of the smaller but still important contributions you make to projects. Finally, maintaining your own portfolio allows you to track those types of contribution that can't appear in a version control system, such as acting as a volunteer coordinator at a community event or mentoring new contributors. Maintaining your own record of all types of contributions makes it very easy to share your contribution portfolio with prospective employers.

Portfolio as Resume?

It is important to stress, however, that despite what many in our industry would like to believe, at *no point* does this portfolio of FOSS contributions replace a resume; it supplements it. A curriculum vitae (CV) or resume shows prospective employers two things: what you've done for past professional positions and what difference you made with those actions. This last point—the difference you made—is very important to communicate to prospective employers. They don't want new team members who have simply done things. They want team members who have done the right things, for the right reasons, and moved the entire team and company forward in some way: someone who made a difference.

While your resume will show your potential employer what you've done, your portfolio reveals how you did it. This is important, of course, but it's not as important as the what. That's because every team has its own particular preference for the how. Your portfolio may show them that you can create effective technical documentation for multiple audiences, but your resume will show them that your documentation reduced contact to the company call center, saving tens of thousands of dollars in support representative time in the first year alone. Therefore, don't give in to the trend to replace your resume with a portfolio. By preparing both, you'll make a strong and positive impact on potential employers.

FOSS Benefits to Your Personal Network

When you mention the word "networking" to many in software development, often they'll do one of two things. Either they'll start telling you about this one time they had to fix their family's router, run their own DNS server, or brought down the entire work subnet because of a typo. Or, if they realize that by "networking" you mean interfacing with other humans, they may blanch and start nervously scanning the room for the closest exit.

Unfortunately, much of our popular and technological culture has trained us to think of networking as an Intimidating Event: a bunch of people gather in a room, shake hands, introduce themselves, and then say smarmy things to each other to drum up new business leads or sell something. While, yes, this sort of thing can qualify as networking, it's more of the exception than the rule. At its most basic, just as computer networking is simply a method for computers to communicate, human networking is simply people communicating with other people. That's it. It doesn't require a special event and it doesn't require special skills or tools beyond what's required to interact with the clerk at your local shop.

Besides some of the negative connotations and misinformation under which many of us work where networking is concerned, there's also the problem that a lot of us are more comfortable interfacing with computers than with other people. Our educations are focused more around solving equations, diagraming sentences, or memorizing dates than about how to hold extemporaneous conversations with our fellow humans. Communicating well requires practice, intention, and attention. If you haven't had the training or opportunities to get that practice, then that communication can be a very scary and uncomfortable thing to approach at first. Don't worry: it gets better once you start getting that practice.

If it's so difficult and uncomfortable for many people to network with others, why should they bother? What's in it for them?

You've probably heard the old phrase, "It's not what you know, it's whom you know." This is networking in an oversimplified nutshell. As you progress through your career, the people you meet along the way can have a marked impact (hopefully in a good way). This doesn't necessarily mean they'll hand you a job, though that does sometimes happen. The most important benefits of these relationships are the discussions, introductions, and information sharing that happen in them. The information could be a pointer to a new technology that will solve a problem that's been vexing you, a what-if question that leads to the launch of a new product, an introduction to a new collaborator or mentor, or a lead on a new position. These benefits and more can come from building and maintaining collegial professional relationships. More than any technology you will ever use or create, the relationships you foster will help you thrive in your career.

Free and open source project participation provides the opportunity for you to meet a broader variety of people than you're likely to in your day-to-day professional life. Many projects include contributors from all over the world and of all culture, skill, and experience types. Contributing to and becoming a member of the communities around these projects gives you instant and easy networking. Simply by listening to and respecfully engaging with the people in the community, you have successfully networked. Congratulations! That wasn't so bad, was it? That's because participation in a FOSS project provides a ready-made shared context and conversation starter. It's very easy to open a dialogue with a stranger when you know that they share an interest and are working toward the same goals as you.

The relationships formed through contributing to free and open source projects may be the most valuable and lasting benefit. These are people who can be there for you when you need advice, feedback, collaborators, or just a good laugh.

Benefit from Preparation

Now that you have a better idea of how contributing to FOSS can benefit your life and your career, there's one more thing to do before you can start looking for a project to contribute to: learn the lay of the land. Your project hunting will go a lot better if you know what files and social structures to look for. The next chapter will prepare you with everything you need to get started.

CHAPTER 3

Prepare to Contribute

You've probably already figured out that contributing to free and open source isn't quite as easy as slinging some code at a project. After all, if it were that easy, there wouldn't be any need for this book. While the steps required for contribution can vary by project and by type of contribution, they generally follow this sort of progression:

1. Realize you want to contribute

2. Find a project

3. Find a task

4. Set up your environment

5. Work on your contribution

6. Submit your contribution

7. Receive feedback and iterate on your contribution

8. Contribution accepted!

9. GOTO 1

You've already realized you want to contribute, otherwise you wouldn't be reading these words. Congratulations on completing step 1 of the process! Look at how far you've come already!

Before we get started finding a project and a task for your first contribution, there are some concepts and terms that you should know. Learning these now will make it much easier to understand what you're seeing when you're reviewing projects. Think of this chapter as setting up some familiar guideposts on your path toward your first contribution.

Ways to Contribute

Throughout most of its history, when people have spoken about contributing to free and open source software, they've mostly meant making programming changes. This led many people to believe that contributions are all about the code, and non-coders are neither needed nor welcome.

Nothing could be further from the truth!

Free and open source software is...well...*software*, so naturally rather a lot of code is involved. But anyone who's ever used software (all of you) realize that there's more to a successful software project than simply the code behind it. There's user interface and user experience design, and documentation as well. That documentation and user interface may require translation to other languages. All of this—code, user interface, documentation—requires testing and review for potential bugs and for stylistic consistency. Testing—either by the team or by end users—leads to bug reports. Bug reports mean that someone needs to triage those bugs to determine reproducibility and severity. And, of course, none of this is possible if there aren't people who are dedicated to organizing and managing the entire process, or people whose focus is to spread the word about and market the software.

To help you visualize the many different ways you might contribute to FOSS, check the tasks below that you think you could do for a project:

☐ Programming (any language)	☐ Accessibility design
☐ UI design	☐ UX design
☐ Web design	☐ Graphic design
☐ Documentation writing	☐ Documentation editing
☐ Translation (any language)	☐ Code testing
☐ User interface testing	☐ Accessibility testing
☐ Bug triage	☐ Release management
☐ Project management	☐ Community management
☐ Event organization and coordination	☐ Public relations and outreach
☐ Marketing	☐ Security review and testing

While this list has a lot of items, it's not complete. Some projects may have needs that aren't represented here. For instance, an open hardware FOSS project may need people who understand electrical engineering, while an open education project needs contributors who have a strong pedagogical background to write and review lesson plans.

Please don't feel you have nothing to contribute to free and open source software if you aren't a programmer. As you can see from the list above, FOSS requires many more skills than simply coding. There's a place for everyone to contribute in free and open source.

Common Project and Community Roles

As you saw in the chart in the previous section, the world of free and open source software needs many different skill sets to create successful projects. It also needs people to take on several different roles. Often you'll find a single person who has taken on a number of roles (especially in smaller projects); other times a project has multiple people taking on a single role to share the responsibility. However it ends up organized in the project, several roles are always at work at any one time.

What exactly are these roles? You've probably already guessed that they vary from project to project, but they typically fall into a few fairly standard categories. Academic authors *Walt Scacchi [Sca07]* and *Y. Ye and K. Kishida [YK03]* found it useful to use *the onion metaphor* to describe the categories of roles in free and open source software projects, where the most active and/or invested roles of the community are in the center, and the level of activity/investiture decreases as you work your way outward through the layers of the onion. Following is an example of a generalized onion model for free and open source community roles:

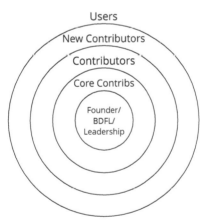

We'll go into a description of each of these roles in a moment, but first it's worth reinforcing that there's more than one way to organize a project, leading to different roles or categories of roles. Which roles a project has and needs are dictated by the project's technical and community needs and its governance structure, not by implied external pressures nor by best practices.

Therefore, for any given project, you may not see all of these roles represented. They are, however, the ones most commonly found in FOSS.

At the core of nearly every project, you find the leadership. While the project founder often is a part of the leadership, it's not uncommon that the founder has gone on to other things and left the project in the capable hands of other people. Sometimes a founder takes on the role *Benevolent Dictator For Life*, or as its more commonly known, BDFL. If the project has a BDFL, then when someone says, "The buck stops here," the role of "here" is played by the BDFL. This person has final say in and can veto all decisions. Typically, though, all leaders of FOSS projects—BDFL or otherwise—work toward consensus rather than impose their authority (hence the *benevolent* part of the title).

One step removed from the core of the community onion, you'll find the *core contributors*. These are typically the most senior or most experienced people in the project. Usually few in number, they provide guidance and mentorship for all other community members, and each one of them is a holder of a *commit bit*. This means they have the authority to approve a contribution (commit) to be merged into the main repository of the project. Having a commit bit is a big responsibility, and it's only given to the most trusted community members. If a core contributor gives you advice or feedback, you can trust that it comes from a place of experience and should be heeded.

Next in the onion are the non-core contributors. These folks provide somewhat regular contributions to the project and are fairly actively involved in most of the discussions. Frequently these contributors pitch in to review contributions from others, as well as provide advice and mentoring for newer contributions. While the BDFL and core contributors may be the heart of the project, these non-core contributors are the lifeblood.

Your onion layer is next! New contributors are, yes, contributors like those in the previous layer, but you're a special group that deserves a layer of your own. New contributors like you are still in their apprenticeship, still learning the ropes of how to operate within the project and its community. Given time and practice, you and the others in your layer will transition to being normal contributors and will be able to provide advice and mentoring for the new contributors who come after you. Projects that pay attention to their new contributor layer—making sure that it's easy for people to join that layer, the layer is well-populated, and these people are given the support necessary to become successful contributors—typically have very strong communities. These projects aren't as common yet, but they're worth seeking out.

On the outer layer of the onion are the users of the project. These folks are just as important as any other layer of the community. Without people using the project, there isn't much reason for the project to exist at all. Users also provide invaluable feedback, bug reports, and feature ideas to help keep the project alive and evolving. If the project starts adding features that the users didn't ask for or don't agree with, it might be a red flag that the leadership way down in the core of the onion has lost sight of what the project is about and what the users need. The project's vitality depends upon meeting the needs of the users and helping to solve their problems. In that way, the users are possibly the most important layer of all.

These are just the most common roles found in free and open source projects, but knowing these few should help you navigate the hierarchy of most of the projects you'll interact with as you enter the world of FOSS contributing.

Files You Should Know About Before You Start

Before you start searching for and reviewing potential projects for your contribution, you should have some familiarity with what files and features you may see. Not all of the files mentioned here exist in all projects, but they're common enough that knowing about them makes it much easier for you to navigate projects.

Most of these files are located in the root directory of a project, but once in a while, you come across a project that placed these files elsewhere. If you don't see one or more of these files in the root directory, see whether the project has a docs or similarly named documentation directory. You may find the file you're looking for there. It's also possible, again, that the file simply does not exist in that project.

README

Typically the very first thing you see for a project is its README file. This is the project's face to the world. The README file tells you the name of the project and what it's intended to do, giving you a quick snapshot to see whether it's a project that might be useful or interesting to you.

The contents of README files vary. Some projects use the file simply to name the project and point you to other resources. Others include those other resources—installation instructions, developer setup, example usage—in the README file itself. The contents of this file are entirely up to the project.

Regardless of the contents, the README file should be your first stop when you visit any project. It can give you a very good sense of what the project is and where to look for more information about it.

LICENSE (also COPYING)

The LICENSE file (also spelled LICENCE) declares the terms under which folks are permitted to use, modify, and distribute the project. This file is also sometimes called COPYING, particularly for projects that use a version of the GNU Public License (GPL),[1] but the purpose remains the same.

As you recall from *The Foundations and Philosophies of Free and Open Source*, if a project is not licensed under an OSI-approved license,[2] it cannot call itself an "open source" project. Doing so violates the definition of the term "open source." If a project is not licensed at all, then it is not "open source;" it is merely "source available." Furthermore, those who use or distribute projects that have no license are infringing on the copyright of the project's creators and putting themselves at risk of legal action.

It's only through that LICENSE file that a project can be "open source," and only through that LICENSE file that the project can legally be used, modified, and distributed. If you come across an interesting project that isn't licensed at all or has a license that isn't OSI-approved, be very careful before you contribute to it and throw yourself into a complicated and suspect copyright situation.

CONTRIBUTING

As a first-time contributor to a project, the CONTRIBUTING (also sometimes called CONTRIBUTORS) file is your best friend and bosom buddy, one you disregard at your peril. The CONTRIBUTING file sets out how the project prefers to receive contributions, the requirements and parameters a contribution must meet to be accepted into the project.

When you make a contribution to a project—whether it's your first contribution or your forty-first—always follow everything that the CONTRIBUTING file tells you to do. If you have any questions about its contents, always ask the community before you proceed. Once you receive an answer, be a good citizen and update the CONTRIBUTING file with the new information.

There's no standard format or contents for a CONTRIBUTING file. Each project includes what it thinks its contributors need to know about its particular

---

1.   http://gplv3.fsf.org
2.   https://opensource.org/licenses

contribution process. Some projects have separate contributor guidelines depending on the type of contribution. For instance, the Apache HTTPD web server has separate guidelines for reporting bugs, for contributing code patches, and for contributing documentation.[3] Other projects have all instructions in a single CONTRIBUTING file. The Public Speaking Resource project[4] handles their contribution guidelines in this way. There's no way to predict what contribution guidelines a project will emphasize or what processes a project follows, so always be sure to look for a CONTRIBUTING file before you get started with your contribution.

If a project does not yet have a CONTRIBUTING file, but you want to make a contribution, what do you do then? For starters, you can look at past contributions to see how those were implemented and handled. Once you have that information, ask the community. "I'm going to make a contribution in *this way*. Is that OK?" If you always verify before simply tossing a contribution to the project, you'll always have a much better chance of your contribution being accepted. Once you've verified the process with the community and made your contribution, be a community superhero by writing it up in the first version of the project's CONTRIBUTING file. You'll be doing the community and its future contributors a huge favor, and you'll rack up yet another contribution.

Code of Conduct

The Code of Conduct (CoC) is a document that—thankfully—is appearing in more and more projects every year. The CoC sets forth the types of behavior that are both welcome and unwelcome in that project community, the consequences for unwelcome behavior, and where and how community members can report it. The intention of the CoC is to encourage behavior that creates a welcoming and safe place for all contributors, regardless of their gender, race, religious beliefs, age, or other characteristics and to provide recourse to those who have been victims of or witness to unwelcome behaviors. The existence of a Code of Conduct is a sign that a project values the safety of its community and welcomes contributors of all stripes.

Implementing a Code of Conduct on a project often is the cause of a lot of (sometimes not very friendly) conversation across the community. Because of that, the document is rarely the same across projects. To appease community members who are nervous about applying any limitations on interactions, some projects create a very minimal, "Be excellent to each other" Code of Conduct. Others create detailed documents that list behavior expectations,

---

3.   https://httpd.apache.org/dev/
4.   https://github.com/vmbrasseur/Public_Speaking

examples of unwelcome behavior, and enforcement instructions. While there's no standard for a project Code of Conduct, many projects now use some derivative of the Contributor Covenant,[5] originally created by Coraline Ada Ehmke.[6]

A Code of Conduct is a valuable document, but it's only as strong and as useful as its enforcement. Without a community that stands by the words in the document, a CoC is no more than a writing exercise. When first viewing a project and its community, it's usually difficult to tell whether it's able to enforce its CoC in an effective and empathetic way. This shouldn't stop you from contributing to or joining a community. Having a Code of Conduct at all is a sign that the community is at least willing to do the right thing, a sign that is very welcome and welcoming to prospective community members.

Styleguides

It's probably no surprise to hear that free and open source software projects often have Very Strong Opinions™ on how things should be done, at least on their turf. We'll get into some of those Opinions in *Make a Contribution*. For now it's enough to know that these Opinions exist, and submitting a contribution that ignores those Opinions is a good way to irritate the project maintainers and community.

Projects that have these Very Strong Opinions usually take the time to codify them in *styleguides*. Depending on the project, you may find a styleguide for programming, for writing, for graphic design... It all depends upon the needs and preferences of the project. Sometimes these guides are included directly in the CONTRIBUTING file, other times they're standalone documents. Whichever way they're implemented, you must always read and follow these guidelines if they exist.

Knowing that styleguides usually spring from project-specific Very Strong Opinions, you probably won't be surprised to hear there's no standard at all for them. You never know what will or won't be included in a styleguide, so it's very important to read them (assuming they exist for a project). Sometimes you'll see styleguides reused between projects or used as a basis for a project's own styleguide. For instance, many projects use the Google Styleguides[7] for their coding guidelines. Others, like the OpenStack family of projects, rely on

---

5. https://www.contributor-covenant.org
6. https://where.coraline.codes
7. https://github.com/google/styleguide

documentation styleguides such as that from IBM.[8] Until you check the styleguide, you won't know what style the project prefers for its contributions.

If a project does not have any sort of styleguide, it doesn't mean that the project lacks those Very Strong Opinions. It's more likely that they simply haven't yet gotten around to writing down those Opinions. Therefore, as you work through your contribution, try to note any stylistic preferences the project maintainers express. Once you've completed your contribution, you have yet another opportunity to don your FOSS superhero cape by writing up the project's stylistic preferences in their very first styleguide(s) and then linking to it in the CONTRIBUTING file.

Other Handy Files You May See

Those were the files you're most likely to encounter when browsing free and open source projects, but a few more are relatively popular, particularly in older or very well-established projects.

The INSTALL or INSTALLATION file is pretty much exactly what you would expect: instructions for how to install and optionally configure the project for use. This file is more common in projects that use make[9] for compiling and installing the software, but there's no reason it couldn't be included in any project (and it often is).

CHANGES or CHANGELOG is, again, fairly self-explanatory. This file contains a human-readable summary of all of the releases for the software and the changes that comprise each. The CHANGES file can be very handy if you're trying to determine whether the version of the software you're using includes a certain bug fix. It's also helpful for new contributors to see the development trajectory of the project.

The AUTHORS file is becoming less common in free and open source projects as they instead rely on version control logs to fulfill a similar purpose. It's still common enough (and valuable enough a tool) to warrant mention. The AUTHORS file lists all people or entities/companies who have made copyrightable contributions to the software. This file may include contact information for these people, but since that can violate a contributor's privacy, this information isn't often included anymore. Having a single, canonical list of copyright holders for the software can simplify copyright statements (that can now say merely, "Copyright 2018, The Authors") and also ease the process of changing a project's license. All copyright holders agree to provide their contributions

---

8. https://docs.openstack.org/doc-contrib-guide/writing-style/general-writing-guidelines.html

9. https://www.gnu.org/software/make/

under a certain license; changing it requires that they all approve to relicense their contributions. Without a list of all copyright holders, this already complex relicensing process can become nightmarish.

Issue Tracking

One of the key characteristics of free and open source software projects is that they are just that: *projects*. As projects, some form of project management is usually required to make sure all development proceeds smoothly. One of the most important of these is the *issue tracker*.

Issue tracking, bug tracking, ticketing system... Different terms but all the same concept: an issue tracker is where a project *tracks* individual *issues* in the project. Yeah, I know, with functionality like that, how did they ever come up with the name "issue tracker?" It's a mystery. Jokes aside, issue trackers are vital for making sure the project knows what is going on, when, and by whom.

The features of issue trackers vary by tracker provider, and many projects don't even use all of the features available. Some projects use the tracker solely for logging bugs in the software. Others use it for bug tracking, feature requests, support questions, design discussions, team conversations and debates... It all depends on the needs and workflow of the project.

The only wrong way to use a project's issue tracker is "anything different from how the project uses it." Don't inject your own preferences or workflow into a project's issue tracker. Sometimes a project documents its issue workflow. If it does, follow it. If it doesn't, have a look at completed ("closed") issues to see which workflow was used for them. As always: ask the community if you have any questions or even just to verify your assumptions. It's better to ask now than to do the wrong thing and make a lot more work for you and for the community.

Common Communication Routes

Since nearly every free and open source project has contributors spread all over the world, communication is vital to success. Over the decades, FOSS has evolved a series of tried and true communication routes that enable efficient, persistent, and effective communication across a variety of use cases. These routes fall into three basic categories: entirely asynchronous (email, issue tracking), semi-asynchronous (real-time chat), and synchronous (audio/video calls, in-person meetups). *Interact with the Community* goes into detail about each of these communication routes.

For some FOSS projects, the selection and use of communication routes fall into that bucket of Very Strong Opinions that I mentioned previously. Each project uses their own combination of routes and process to meet their own needs, so make sure you seek out documentation and advice about this before you participate in any project discussions. Incorrectly using communication routes is a common way new contributors leave a poor first impression on a community they hope to join.

If you're going to participate in FOSS, you need to be comfortable with email. Many free and open source projects rely heavily on mailing lists. A mailing list allows a project with contributors distributed across time zones to receive and reply to conversations when it's most convenient for them. Mailing lists also allow people to take the time to think through and craft their responses for a discussion. This is particularly helpful and welcoming to community members whose primary language is not the same as that of the project. These people make insightful and valuable contributions to discussions but require a little more time to translate those thoughts into, for instance, English from Polish. Add to that the archivability and searchability of email threads, and mailing lists become a powerful tool for collaboration in free and open source software projects.

While mailing lists can allow for rich and nuanced conversations, there's nothing like a real-time chat for building comraderie and helping to coordinate a complex process. Many FOSS projects use a real-time chat system of some sort. Internet Relay Chat (IRC)[10] is a very popular option, but far from the only one. Other options include Matrix,[11] RocketChat,[12] and Mattermost.[13] The selection and use of a real-time chat system has taken on nearly religious significance in some free and open source software communities of late. Rest assured that no matter what chat system is in use by the projects in which you participate, a great deal of conversation (and possibly arguments) went into its selection and maintenance.

Respect the communication routes chosen and used by the project, as well as rules and guidelines they've set forth for their use. If you strongly object to the routes a project uses, rather than complain about it (passive-aggressively or otherwise), I advise you to select a different project to which to contribute. Your complaints will fall on deaf ears, and you'll simply alienate the community you'd wish to join. Respect their choices and the process that went into making them.

---

10. https://opensource.com/life/16/6/irc
11. https://matrix.org
12. https://rocket.chat
13. https://about.mattermost.com

Contributor License Agreement/Developer Certificate of Origin

A few free and open source software projects require all contributors to agree to either a Contributor License Agreement or a Developer Certificate of Origin before their contributions can be merged and distributed with the software. While the number of projects that require this is still relatively small, it's increasing every year, as more projects join free and open source software foundations. Before you get started, it's worth knowing about these documents and how they might impact your contributions.

Some projects—especially but not exclusively, those developed under the aegis of a large corporation—require all contributors to sign a *Contributor License Agreement* (CLA). A CLA is a document resplendent with intellectual property implications and therefore, a controversial matter for some free and open source software practitioners.

The contents and prescriptions vary by CLA, but basically, one exists to make sure that you (or your company, if you're contributing on their behalf) have the right to share your contributions, agree that the project has a license to alter, distribute, and administer those contributions, and you agree that you will never revoke that license. Sometimes the document also includes a transfer of copyright from the contributor to the project or project's organizing body. The intention of the CLA is to minimize potential legal complications of distributing the work, as well as to potentially make it easier to change license.

As mentioned, CLAs are controversial for some people and projects. Many object that the requirement to sign a CLA before making a contribution not only slows down the entire contribution process and adds administrative overhead to the process, but also discourages many people from contributing at all. Other people object to the idea of signing over their copyright to another entity (again, that's not a feature of all CLAs).

Recently, the *Developer Certificate of Origin* (DCO)[14] has become a more popular alternative to CLAs. A short and simple document, the DCO ostensibly achieves the results of a CLA without the administrative overhead or related slowdown in contributions. A DCO relies upon a contributor signing their contribution using the -s or --signoff flags of the git version control system. This signing denotes that they have the right to distribute their contribution and do so under the same conditions as the project license. This means that the

---

14. https://developercertificate.org

DCO can only be applied to contributions that can be committed to the project's git version control system...assuming the project uses git at all. If the project uses Subversion, CVS, or another version control system, it may not be able to use the DCO. So the DCO is not the right solution for all projects nor all contributions, but some projects find it a welcome change from CLAs.

You're Ready to Find a Project

OK, you're now equipped with the guideposts you need for a very basic navigation of a free and open source project. The next step is a fun one: Find a project where you can make your first contribution!

CHAPTER 4

Find a Project

The question I hear most often from people wanting to contribute to free and open source software is, "How can I find a project to contribute to?" or even just, "Where do I start?" You may have heard of open source and know that it's possible to contribute. You may even know why you want to contribute and what you want to get out of it, but it's rare for people to have recognized that a lot of thought needs to go into the choice of where to contribute. Mostly, what all potential new contributors know is that they want to contribute in some way. You're probably in this camp, and that's better than OK—it's great. You've passed the first milestone for contribution: wanting to contribute at all. The second milestone is finding the project that's right for you.

Finding a free and open source project to which to contribute isn't as simple as choosing a random bug in a random project. You can do it this way, sure, but you're unlikely to be successful or to have a positive experience. Before you dive in, give yourself a better chance of success: take the time to find a project that matches *your* goals and values. This, of course, implies you can actually articulate your goals and requirements, so that's where we'll start.

I won't lie: defining your goals and requirements and finding the right first project can take some time to do properly, but it's a very good investment. What isn't a good investment? Spending days, weeks, or months trying to contribute to a project that isn't a good fit for you.

Set Your Goals

You may know that you want to contribute to free and open source software in some way, but can you put your finger on exactly why you want to do this? The answer is a lot harder than it seems at first. Some people may answer, "to get experience," or "I believe software should be Free," or "my teacher/mentor told me it would be a good idea." While these might be motivations, they're not goals. These statements are vague and difficult to pin down, therefore, it's also difficult to tell whether you've succeeded in them. Goals must be specific and actionable, otherwise they're just smoke in the wind.

After reading the past few chapters, you may have some more thoughts about why you want to contribute to free and open source software. *The Foundations and Philosophies of Free and Open Source* covered the philosophies underlying FOSS. These may resonate well with your own philosophies, values, and ethics in such a way that cultivating and spreading these philosophies may factor into your personal goals for contributing to free and open source. *What Free and Open Source Can Do for You* detailed some of the many professional benefits you might reap when contributing to FOSS. Some of these benefits may suit your own purposes, and may even have inspired you to think of personal benefits that were not mentioned (it was far from an exhaustive list).

Regardless of whether you feel you have a firm grasp on your reasons and goals for contributing, collect your thoughts and write them down. Doing so not only gives you a snapshot of your current state of mind, but it also gives you something to which you can refer later on. You might revisit your goals to update them, or—if you're having a bad day—to remind yourself why you're putting up with all of this in the first place.

Grab your favorite writing device and a cup of a tasty beverage and sit down to collect those thoughts. Give yourself permission to write anything that comes to mind, in whatever order those thoughts fall out of your head. There are no wrong answers or thoughts here, so collect them all in this brainstorm-ing session without passing judgment or trying to organize them. The time to organize is later, after you've gotten all of your goal-related thoughts out of your brain and into the open where you can view them all at once. An example of a possible brainstorm is shown in the figure on page 41.

Once you've collected all of your goal-related thoughts, set them aside for a short while before you move on to the next step. Allowing your brain to rest will help give you a better perspective when you start to organize your thoughts, and may even allow a few straggling thoughts to bubble up and be captured in your brainstorm. So take a break: mow the lawn, do the dishes, play a game with your kids, watch a movie, or even just sleep on it.

OK, is your brain all rested? Good, because now we get to the hard part: taking all of those thoughts and organizing, consolidating, and focusing them into a list of goals.

Look at your list of thoughts. Are there any that are vague? Expand on them until they're specific. Are there any that are similar? Collect them together.

Goal brainstorming:

What do I want to get out of this? Why am I even doing it?

- ~~*the teacher told me to*~~
- ~~*I don't want to fail the assignment*~~
- *practice my CSS*
- *I don't know any Javascript and want to learn some*
- *meet cool new people!*
- *we had a unit on accessibility in UI design, could I learn more about that?*
- *it would be really cool if something I designed were used by a lot of people*
- *could I put that in my portfolio?*
- *would force me finally to learn how to use git*
- *does command line stuff count as UI? could I design that?*
- *learn how to work with programmers better*
- *learn from experienced designers*
- *do hardware projects need designers? could I do some industrial designy-type things?*
- *get better at writing*

As you review them, make sure you understand the why behind every thought. If there are any for which you have no discernable reason beyond, "it seemed like a good idea at the time," disqualify them from the goal process and set them aside. Iteratively refine and collect your thoughts into categories until you've consolidated them into the few core things you would like to achieve by contributing to free and open source software. How many of these core goals constitute "a few" is up to you and your needs. Each goal should be specific, concise, and actionable, something you can state to someone and have them immediately understand what you hope to achieve. Vague goals are difficult to make progress on. For instance, "Practice programming" is a vague goal. Programming what? In what language? How will you tell when you've accomplished this goal? On the other hand, "Become more proficient and fluent at server-side Javascript" is specific and actionable. This is a goal that is easy for you to focus on and just as easy to see whether you're making progress toward it. See the figure on page 42.

My goals:

- *Gain greater proficiency in CSS*
- *Start learning Javascript*
- *Learn how to use git with design artefacts*
- *Improve the accessibility of at least one UI*
- *Practice communicating and collaborating with programmers*
- *Write a design proposal*
- *Find a designer mentor*
- *Add at least one new piece to my portfolio*

Remember: These are your goals, sprung from your own thoughts and needs. While they may possibly resemble those of others, these goals are entirely unique to you. Be true to your personal needs and goals; don't simply take the goals handed to you by a teacher or mentor. Own your goals, take responsibility for meeting them, and you are much more likely to be successful in your FOSS contributions.

An advantage of these being your own, personal goals is that you are free to change them as needed. These goals are not carved in stone. As your life and career evolve, your goals should as well. Revisit this page from time to time and review the goals you've written here. Do your goals still ring true? Do they still meet the needs of your life? If not, how should your goals change and, more importantly, why? If necessary, go through the entire exercise again from brainstorm to goals to ensure that you're still targeting goals that are good for you, your life, and your career. Don't spend years driving yourself toward goals that no longer serve your needs.

Collect Your Requirements

You have your goals figured out, so you're ready to go out into the FOSS world and find a project to contribute to, right? Nope, not quite yet. Your goals are only one piece of the puzzle. You also need to know your personal requirements for the project you select. Think of these as the criteria the project must meet to be a good fit for you. Contributing to a project that isn't a good fit is like wearing the wrong size shoes: They may look cute, but after taking a few steps, you'll be in quite a lot of pain. To maximize your chances of success with your first contribution, take a few minutes to figure out what size you should wear.

What do I mean by *requirements*? These are project characteristics that meet your own particular needs. Only you know what sort of characteristics are required for you to be successful, but I'll list some of the most common things that people should consider when looking for a free and open source project to which to contribute.

Skills

For starters, what are your skills? What can you offer to a project? Are you a great writer or editor? How about translation? Graphic design? User experience specialist? Know certain programming languages? Have experience with electronics? Maybe you have experience managing people, writing technical specifications or grants, or organizing events? All these skills and more are in demand for free and open source projects and communities. Take a few minutes to write down all of your skills that may be potentially relevant to contributing to FOSS.

Skills I bring to the party

- *graphic design training*
- *fluent in Spanish and English*
- *some experience with branding*
- *very good at HTML*
- *know some CSS (want to get better!)*
- *did well in the intro to programming class*
- *good with InDesign and Photoshop*
- *leader of local graphic design student meetup*

Those are the things you can do, but what about the things that interest you?

Interests

You're much more likely to enjoy and stick with contributing to free and open source software if you're working on a project that interests you, rather than working on the first one you come across. Besides enjoying it more, if you choose a project for an interest you already know something about, then you have *domain knowledge*. This is knowledge about how things operate in that interest area. For instance, if you sew, knit, or fix cars, then you already know all of the terminology for sewing, knitting, or car repair. If you find a project related to one of these areas of interest, you'll more easily understand what the project does and perhaps even how it works.

There's a free and open source project for every hobby and interest area. When most people think of FOSS they immediately think of operating systems (Linux), infrastructure, databases, or web development. If these are your interests, you're in luck, since there's always a lot of work that needs to be done on these projects. But there are also projects for ham radio, sewing, game development, digital art, machine learning, astrophysics, geography, 3-D printing, education... The list goes on and on.

What sorts of things interest you? What are your hobbies? What classes did you enjoy in school? Take a few more minutes to write down all of your areas of interest.

Interests! Hobbies! Curious about...!

- dogs
- soccer
- graphic design
- pixel art
- video games
- board games
- digital painting
- Spanish comic books
- running
- road biking
- fighting climate change
- BBQ
- bass guitar

Time Availability

Another very important requirement is your time availability. A single parent with three young children will have much different time availability than a second year university student. Before you start looking for a project to which to contribute, be honest with yourself about how much time you think you can devote to contributing to free and open source software. Some projects have a much steeper learning curve than others, so if you have only a little bit of time, you may need to limit your project selection to one that has a reputation as being very supportive of and helpful to new contributors.

No matter which project you choose, it's very possible to contribute even if you have only a couple hours a week to devote to it. Every contribution is valuable, even the small ones. Be realistic about your time investment and take on only what you can manage. You can always ramp up your contributions later should more time become available to you.

Goals

The goals you defined earlier are also a part of your requirements for project selection. It doesn't make a lot of sense to contribute to a project if it's not going to help you move toward your goals in some way. Take the time to revisit them if it's been a while since you last did.

Skills, interests, time availability, and goals. These are your specific requirements, and they are unique. If you compare your lists to anyone else's, you may find some overlap, but you're more likely to find more differences. These requirements are yours and yours alone, and only you can define them. Others may be able to help you brainstorm or refine your lists, but no one can tell you what your personal requirements are.

And remember: all of these requirements can and will change over time as your life situation evolves and professional experience grows. Don't be afraid to revisit these requirements and refresh or alter them later. Doing so can help provide a lot of clarity if you're ever feeling a bit lost about where to look for your next project or challenge.

Collect Candidate Projects

OK! You have goals! You have interests! You have requirements! Now all you need is a project. How hard could it be, right? Welllll…

As I mentioned in *The Foundations and Philosophies of Free and Open Source*, millions and millions of free and open source projects are in existence today. How are you supposed to apply those goals/interests/requirements to millions of projects? Answer: by limiting the pool of candidates.

Start by looking at the projects you already use and enjoy. If you're a Linux user, then you probably have a lot of free and open source software projects that you use on a daily basis. Blender,[1] GIMP,[2] KDE[3] or GNOME,[4] and all of the tools associated with them are all FOSS projects. But daily use of free and open source isn't limited just to those who run Linux on their machines.

---

1. https://www.blender.org
2. https://www.gimp.org
3. https://www.kde.org
4. https://www.gnome.org

FOSS projects are everywhere: Drupal,[5] Moodle,[6] Visual Studio Code,[7] iTerm,[8] and more! Look at the software you use every day, then check to see whether it's a FOSS project. While these large and very visible projects may not be the best starting point for someone new to FOSS contributions, they may have smaller satellite projects (such as libraries, plugins, extensions) that are perfect for someone who's just starting out.

Even if the software itself is not free or open source, it's possible that an ecosystem has sprung up around it that is. For instance, if you use the Unity[9] engine for game or video development, you'll find that a lot of the plugins for it are released under OSI-approved licenses. If you're a Mac or an iOS developer, you're probably using tools or libraries that are released as open source. Nearly all browsers allow for third-party extensions now. Many of those extensions are available as FOSS projects. So take the time to inspect your software and its ecosystems. You're likely to find you've been using and enjoying free and open source software and didn't even know it.

All of those interests you listed previously make for a great starting point for locating free and open source projects. Open your favorite web browser, fire up your favorite web search engine, and type an interest name followed by the words "open source" into the search field. The results will undoubtedly point the way to a lot of FOSS projects that you never knew existed. For instance, if I type woodworking open source into my search engine today, I receive 772,000 search results. sewing open source returns 1,920,000 results. painting open source returns an eye-popping 7,880,000 results from this search engine. Enter each of your interests into a search engine in this way and see whether any intriguing free and open source projects are revealed. If they are, add them to your list of candidates.

Another way to locate interesting free and open source projects is to browse popular version control service providers. As I write this, the most popular of these providers for free and open source software are GitHub,[10] GitLab,[11] and BitBucket,[12] but there are others (including self-hosting by the projects themselves). Most of these services offer a way to explore the public repositories

---

5.   https://www.drupal.org
6.   https://moodle.org
7.   https://code.visualstudio.com
8.   https://iterm2.com
9.   https://unity3d.com
10. https://github.com
11. https://gitlab.com
12. https://bitbucket.org

they serve. Sometimes the service provides a special page for this purpose, highlighting and categorizing projects by topic, programming language, popularity, or some other characteristic. These services and pages can be a great way to discover projects you might not locate otherwise.

Your network and local community can be a great resource for finding free and open source projects to which to contribute. Do you have friends who have contributed to FOSS? How about your social network (Twitter, Facebook, and the like)? Ask them about their experiences and whether they can recommend projects that might be a good fit for you. Nearly as important, ask them whether they've had any bad experiences with projects. It's much better to learn now that a project has a toxic community or is difficult to contribute to than to learn it later the hard way. You can also just put yourself out there on social media and offer your services. "I would like to contribute to a FOSS project! My skills are... Does your project need my help?" I have seen this work to good effect, but the success of this method depends a lot upon the reach of your message. If it doesn't get in front of the right people, you're unlikely to receive many helpful responses.

While you're doing your research to locate candidate projects, simply add them to your list as shown in the figure on page 48. There's no need to research or compare them yet, and it'll be easier to compare them once you have a better idea of the options that exist for you. Also, it could be that a few projects keep reappearing in your searches. The more often you come across a project while doing searches that are targeted toward your requirements, the more likely it is that the project may be a good fit for you. Regardless, invest an hour or two to collect a nice pool of candidate projects and to familiarize yourself with the landscape of free and open source projects that exist in the world.

Select a Project

You've done a lot of work by this point, so the next step may not take you very long. It's time to select a project where you can start contributing. You could do this the old fashioned way by throwing a dart at a dartboard covered in potential projects, or you could do it the smart way by comparing the list of projects you've built with your list of requirements. It's possible that there won't be a single project that meets all of the requirements on your list. That's OK. As long as it meets some of them, you'll still be moving toward your personal goals.

While matching your requirements is a very important feature for any potential project, it's not the only one you should take into consideration.

Candidate projects

- *Inkscape*
- *Scribus*
- *Blender*
- *GIMP*
- *Krita*
- *Godot*
- *Twine*
- *ORX*
- *melonJS*
- *Aseprite*
- *Zuluru*
- *GoldenCheetah*
- *Sonic Pi*
- *HeaterMeter*

There's also the matter of how easy it will be for you to contribute. This will be your first contribution, after all. Why not give yourself the best possible chance of success by choosing a project that makes contributing more straightforward? It may feel like stacking the deck in your favor...and you'd be right. But there's nothing wrong with that, is there? If you start your free and open source software contributions with an easy win, you'll be much more motivated to continue down the path of contributing elsewhere.

Have a look at each project on your list, starting with the documentation. Does the project have a CONTRIBUTING file or similar documentation guiding people through the contribution process? Does it have robust documentation for setting up a developer environment? Are the communication routes for the project documented and active (people who ask questions receive answers)? If so, you may have a good starter project on your hands. Next, have a look at the project's issue tracker. Are there any open bugs or features that you think you might be able to tackle? Maybe some of them are tagged as *Help Wanted, First Timers Only, Newbie, Good First Issue, Up For Grabs*, or some similar flag to highlight them for people like you.

It's certainly not required that a project do all of these things. Thousands of very good projects are out there, supported by healthy communities, that do not meet all of the criteria in the preceding paragraph. However, if you find a project that has implemented even one of those criteria, you'll find that it will make your first time contribution experience much more pleasant than contributing to a project that has not.

Once you've reviewed all of the projects on your list for how easy they may be to contribute to, your choice of starter project may now be obvious to you. If it's not, don't worry. For some people, it's better to explicitly list the pros and cons for each project, then analyze and review them all together this way. There's no right or wrong method for coming to your decision. Do what's best for you and the way your brain works.

Remember, though: when you decide on a starter project, that decision is not carved in stone. You may find that the community is not as welcoming as you hoped, or once you start contributing, you aren't getting what you need out of it. If that's the case, it's perfectly OK to stop contributing there and find another project where you can devote your time. I caution you, though: before you quit, consider whether you might be the problem. In your zeal to contribute, it may be that you're not doing as good of a job as you could in communicating or understanding the contribution process. Ask the project community for feedback, help, and mentoring (just don't expect to be spoon-fed). If these things aren't forthcoming or don't help you feel more comfortable with the project, don't hesitate to move on to something that is a better fit for you.

Select a Task

You have a project! Congratulations! Now you're ready to get started on that first contribution, right? Well…sorta. Before you can make that first contribution, you have to figure out what it will be. You have to decide upon a task.

It could be that you already have something in mind. You may have discovered a bug or typo in documentation, or docs that are missing altogether and you'd like to add. Perhaps there's a bug in the software, something that's been bothering you for a while and which you can easily reproduce. Maybe you use a certain library for a work project, but to continue, you need to add a feature to the library API.

Whatever the task, before you start work on it, search the project's issue tracker to see whether it exists. Don't limit your search purely to open or active issues, either. Search the closed issues to see whether your idea was proposed before, but the project decided not to pursue it for some reason.

If your idea doesn't exist in the issue tracker, open a new issue. This serves two purposes. First, it warns the project that a contribution may be on its way. Second, it allows the project maintainers to review the task and confirm that it's something the project needs or wants. It can be very disheartening to put a lot of work into a contribution only to learn afterward that it's not a good fit for the project, so do take the time to write it up in an issue in advance.

If you don't already have a task in mind, a good source for one is the project's issue tracker. Most every project has one of these, though they may use a different name for it; bug database and ticketing system are two other common names for this. Most of these systems include some way to 'tag' issues to make them easier to categorize and locate. The tags vary from project to project, but often a project has a tag that's used to mark certain issues as suitable for new contributors to tackle. Examples of tags that may mean this are: *easy, starterbug, newbie, help wanted,* or *good first ticket.* If a project tags issues as suitable for new contributors, they usually mention that and what tag to look for in their contributor guide, so look there as well. Whether the project has tagged issues in this way or not, review the issues and select one that looks achievable, considering your personal skillset and experience.

While working on finding a suitable task, never underestimate the power of Just Asking. Do your own research to familiarize yourself with the project, its needs, and its communication routes. Pick the most appropriate route—this will vary by project—and introduce yourself. Let the community know who you are, that you're new and excited to help out, and briefly state your skills so they'll have some idea of your current capabilities. If you already have an issue in mind, let them know which one and verify that it would be appropriate for you to work on. If you haven't chosen an issue yet, ask whether someone can direct you to one or whether you might help someone with a task they're already working on. When you write to the community in this way, please be patient and respectful of their time. They may not be able to reply to you very quickly. It's not personal; it's just that they all have their own lives and obligations to attend to as well and may be many time zones away.

As you filter through tasks to find a good one for you, I encourage you to start small. Yes, you have goals you wish to fulfill through your contributions, but free and open source participation is a marathon, not a sprint. Take the long view, particularly when you're starting out. Small tasks lead to a quicker payoff and better chance of success than trying to tackle a large feature or tricky bug. This payoff takes the form of the endorphin hit you'll get when your first contribution is accepted by the community, and it feels great. The larger and more complicated the task you select, the longer you postpone getting that payoff, so start small. Baby steps are still steps and still move you toward your goal.

Similarly, simple and repetitive tasks not only allow you to contribute quickly, but they also help you make friends and influence people in the community. By taking on these important but less fun tasks, you not only free up the time of more experienced community members, but you also show them that you're willing to dig in and do what it takes to lend a hand and work your way up through the ranks of the community.

What Is "Success"?

All through this chapter I've repeatedly said, "do this thing to maximize your success" or similar statements to that effect, but I've never defined what *success* is.

That's because I don't get to define what success is for you; only *you* can. Without goals, without requirements, you can never truly know whether you're making the right choices for your own needs. Those goals and requirements are very personal things. Your goals will not match my goals; your requirements will not match my requirements; your success will not match my success. Despite that, some general characteristics of your contributions can signal whether you are or are not on the path toward your success:

- You're able to make a first contribution with minimal fuss
- You're welcomed by your first community
- You learn and grow from your experience
- You gain the confidence to help others contribute, too

You will not see all of these characteristics at once. For instance, you won't necessarily have gained the confidence to help others contribute until you've contributed a few times yourself and are more familiar with the process (at least for that project). It's possible to be welcomed by a community before you make your first contribution to it. So if you don't see a particular characteristic, don't worry. It may just be waiting around the next corner. However, if after trying to contribute for a couple of months, you still don't see any of these characteristics, do consider whether the project you've chosen is the right fit for you. Don't be like Don Quixote, tilting at windmills to no end. If you're not making any progress, it's OK to set that project aside, re-collect your notes on project selection, and try another one. You won't meet your goals if you end up a crumpled heap at the foot of a windmill somewhere, so stop tilting at them.

CHAPTER 5

Make a Contribution

At this point, it can be tempting to just jump in and start working on your contribution. For some people and some contributions, this might even be successful, but for the rest of us, it's not usually that easy. Don't worry, though: you can do this, and by the end of this chapter, you'll know what to do to make your contribution successful.

Making your first contribution to a project can be complicated. If the project isn't well documented, if its community isn't very communicative, if your contribution is complex, if you don't have a lot of time or other resources available... Plenty of things could cause your first contribution to go a little less smoothly than you'd wish.

It's OK at this point to pause and think through the process and your contribution before you submit it to the project. Don't dive in headfirst; wade in instead. Basically, there are five large parts to any free and open source contribution:

1. Prepare

2. Craft

3. Test

4. Submit

5. Revise

Let's walk through each part of this process.

Prepare for Your Contribution

There's plenty for you to do even before you can start in on your first contribution. The more you prepare in advance, the more likely it is that your contribution will be well received. There's a reason that *Fail to prepare? Prepare to fail* is such a commonly used phrase: it's true. The time you invest before you dive into your contribution will pay great dividends later on in the process.

Review the Issue Tracker

If you didn't already do so in the prior chapter, invest some time to review the issue or bug tracker for your chosen project (see *Find a Project* for more information about the issue tracker). It's an amazing resource for learning what a project has done in the past, what it's currently trying to accomplish, what it's looking to do in the future, and just as importantly as all those: what it's decided it doesn't need to do at all.

Regardless of whether the project tags its issues as suitable for a new contributor, reviewing the open issues in its issue tracker can lead you to a number of potential contributions. As you skim the issues, look for those that are interesting in some way. Are bugs reported that have bitten you in the past? Maybe there are issues that were opened but have no activity yet, or issues marked as needing work but are not yet assigned to nor claimed by anyone. Picking up tasks that no one else has had the time to do can be a great way to make your mark in a community.

Set Up Your Environment

Creating and testing your contribution usually requires setting up a testing environment of some sort. Often the project has documentation describing how to do this. Sometimes the documentation is the steps to install the project itself. Regardless, you'll need some way to verify that your contribution actually works or looks the way expected and intended.

Once in a great while, you'll find a project that has provided a container or virtual machine image to give you the ideal testing environment. This is quite rare though; it can take a lot of time and effort to maintain those images, and time/effort are two things in very short supply for most projects.

If the project doesn't provide steps to set up a testing environment or otherwise install the software, ask the community for help. It could be that the steps for this are in a less obvious location. If the project does not have documentation for this, take notes while you're setting up your testing environment. Once you're done, convert these notes into documentation (and also your first contribution to the project). Your efforts will help everyone from that point forward.

This testing environment doesn't only apply to code or technical writing contributions. If you're helping with the project website, its user interface, or even performing translations, you need to test your changes before sharing them with the community. Figure out what sort of testing environment you need for your specific type of contribution and make sure it works before you lift a finger to start crafting your contribution.

Text Editors

The workhorse of most FOSS contributions is the text editor. Without a good text editor, it's very difficult to make a contribution at all. It may seem like a simple thing, but it turns out which text editor you use can make a big difference when doing software development.

The two text editors you hear about most in free and open source software development are *vi* (vim) and *emacs*. Both are venerable and beloved to the point of a near-religious rivalry between users of each editor. Both also have well-earned reputations for being difficult to learn. I encourage you to become familiar with them at some point, but it's not necessary to learn either to contribute to an open source project. Other text editors will do just fine.

There are many different text editors out there in the world, but not all of them are good for software development. For instance, while it's possible to edit text in Microsoft Word or Microsoft Notepad, neither of these are suitable editors for software development. The text output of these programs contains control characters that can make your code or documentation unreadable by many other programs. They also use different line endings (carriage returns) than many programs expect, which can cause a lot of problems.

A good text editor for software development outputs nothing except Unicode or ASCII characters. Which editors are available depends on your operating system, but some popular ones are Notepad++,[1] Sublime Text,[2] Atom,[3] Kate,[4] and Geany.[5] If you develop on a Windows system, the WordPad application will work well for most text-based contributions like code or documentation.

There's so much talk about text editors in some open source circles that you might wonder whether it's acceptable to use an integrated development

---

1. https://notepad-plus-plus.org
2. https://www.sublimetext.com
3. https://atom.io
4. https://kate-editor.org
5. https://www.geany.org

environment (IDE) such as Visual Studio Code,[6] Xcode,[7] or Eclipse.[8] The answer is: Yes, you can definitely use an IDE to create your free and open source contributions. Just make sure the end product meets the criteria and styleguide for the project. The bottom line is, the best tool for the job is the one that you can use and that generates the output you need. Don't let anyone tell you otherwise. You do you, honey.

Do Issue Triage

Before jumping in and working on a fix for an issue, pause and do some triage first. In a medical sense, triage is reviewing wounds to determine how severe they are. In a technical sense, it's reviewing issues to confirm you understand the problem, can duplicate it, and that it's not already fixed elsewhere. In many projects, issue triage also includes setting a priority for fixing the issue, but that is not usually possible for new contributors to determine, as they lack the big picture view that more experienced contributors have. You will learn a lot more about triaging bugs in *Make a Difference Without Making a Pull Request*.

Doing issue triage takes time up front, but it saves much more time during implementation of the fix for the issue. Triage allows you to confirm that the issue you selected is still, well, an issue. It could be that the problem was resolved in another commit or that the issue itself is just out of date. Triage also allows you to confirm not only whether the issue can be duplicated, but also that you fully understand the requirements of the fix. This understanding leads to more efficient and effective fixes and a much smoother contribution process.

To triage your issue, you must be able to duplicate it or view it in some way. This usually means using that shiny new testing environment you just set up. Review the issue for the steps to reproduce the problem or any other hints about where to look to view the problem itself. If you're able to reproduce the problem, you have a much better chance of understanding what's going on and where to start looking to solve it.

As you triage your issue, document all of your discoveries: the steps to duplicate the issue, what you expected to see, what you actually did see, and any additional requirements (technical or otherwise) that aren't listed in the issue. Add this to a public note in the issue itself. Think of the issue as a lab

---

6.   https://code.visualstudio.com
7.   https://developer.apple.com/xcode/
8.   https://www.eclipse.org/home/

notebook and you're the scientist seeking a discovery. Documenting everything allows other community members to confirm your work and provide guidance if necessary before you invest a lot of time in crafting a fix for the issue. Documenting your triage notes also helps the next people who look at the issue. Should your triage show that the issue fix is beyond your current skill or interest level, your notes allow the next person who works on the issue to make progress that much more quickly.

Read the Docs (or Write Them)

No matter what, as you're working with issues, make sure you follow the project's workflow for them. This may be documented (in either the CONTRIBUTING file or elsewhere), but often the workflow is a matter of tribal knowledge. If you find this to be the case, ask a community member for advice and guidance before making a clumsy faux pas with issue handling. Once you have that advice and guidance, write it down for posterity. This important documentation can not only help future contributors, but it can also be your first contribution to the project!

Craft Your Contribution

Once you have some idea whether your contribution is needed for the project, you're ready to create it.

The specifics of how you create it naturally will vary depending on the type of contribution: documentation, user experience, design, code, or other types. Each contribution type obviously will have its own creation process.

Whatever that process is, before you start, do double-check whether the project has already defined some guidelines for it. As covered in *Prepare to Contribute*, many projects provide styleguides and contributor instructions. For instance, if your contribution is code, the project may require it to include both unit and integration tests or perhaps that it pass certain linter rules. If documentation, the project may follow a certain writing styleguide such as AP[9] or IBM, or may require contributions to be written in a specific dialect (British English instead of American English, for instance). Website or graphic design contributions may need to stick to the project's branding guide or to an accessibility style guide.[10] Always double-check the contribution guidelines before you get too far with your work. Doing so may save you a lot of time later on.

---

9.   https://www.apstylebook.com
10. http://a11y-style-guide.com

Gotchas

If you haven't spent much time in free and open source yet, you may be blindsided by some topics that you wouldn't think should matter, but for various historical and social reasons matter a great deal. Two of those topics are spaces versus tabs, and tab sizes.

Spaces, Tabs, and Tab-size

The controversy between using tab characters or space characters for indenting your (typically code) contribution often catches new contributors off guard.

A single space character looks more or less the same on every screen, in every text editor, and on every platform.

A single tab character, however, can be interpreted and displayed differently by every text editor. Some editors display a tab as eight spaces, others as four. Most good text editors allow the user to define how many spaces to use when displaying a tab character, also known as "set the tab-size". Some text editors allow the user to enter a tab character but then replace it in the text with space characters equivalent to the user's preferred setting.

So why is this such a big deal?

Many projects value consistency in appearance across all editors and platforms. For them, it's very helpful to know editing a file on Windows will present a display similar to editing it on Linux. This prevents surprises when editing files and allows peoples' brains and eyes to learn where to look on the screen for what information. It provides for a visual consistency in the same way a linter or styleguide provides for consistency in content. Projects that prefer this consistency will dictate that contributions use spaces for indentation. They also will dictate the preferred tab-size or indentation size (usually 4 spaces, but 2 and 8 are sometimes found as well; people who use other sizes might be monsters).

Other projects prefer to allow their contributors to control how their display looks. Contributors who would rather work in a more compact editor window can set their tab-size to 2 spaces, for instance, while contributors who desire a larger visual difference between indent levels can set their tab-size to 4 or 8 spaces. Projects that prefer this visual flexibility will dictate that contributions use tabs instead of spaces for indentation.

Finally, some projects use programming languages, such as Python,[11] where the whitespace is *significant*: If you indent in one of these languages, that

---

11. https://www.python.org

indentation affects the program. And if your indentation is a different size from other peoples' indentations, it can cause a lot of chaos. Paying attention to tabs, spaces, and whitespace is critical to projects that use these programming languages.

While we all end up having our own preferences between spaces and tabs, when contributing, the only right way to do it is that defined by the project. Even if the project's preferences are not your own, always respect and follow the project's rules. If the project to which you're contributing prefers either spaces or tabs, stick to their preference or risk offending the project community and having your contribution rejected. If the project has not expressed a preference, ask the community about it before starting work. If nothing else, you often can default to indenting with spaces with a tab-size of 4.

Clone and Branch

The first step in any contribution is to retrieve a local copy of the repository (*repo*). In git terminology, this local copy is known as a clone, but some hosting services use the term fork instead. In the git contribution process, both words refer to the same step, though the two words can mean different things in a FOSS context.[12]

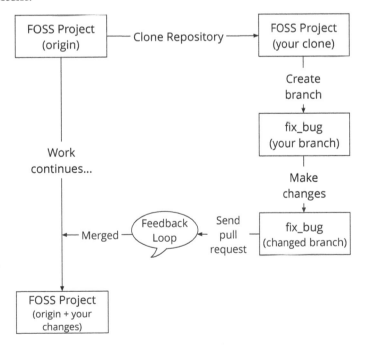

---

12. https://opensource.com/article/17/12/fork-clone-difference

The next step after cloning the repository is to create a branch. When you create a branch, you name it and figuratively plant a flag in the repository to say, "I hereby claim everything from here forward in the name selected for the branch." As long as you stay on that branch, all of your work will be isolated from every other branch. This allows you to work on multiple different issues at once (by creating multiple branches), but most importantly, it prevents you from sharing changes that you don't want to. In the background, a branch is just a named pointer to a certain git commit, but that's a level of detail that you can read up on later if you want.[13] The important part is that a branch is just a pointer, not a copy of the repository. Therefore, branches in git are cheap, quick, and easy to create and destroy. Easy branches are one of the big advantages of git over earlier version control systems like Subversion or CVS.

A common mistake at this point (and one I've made myself in the past) is to start making changes and working directly on this new copy of the repo. While this can be OK, the best practice is instead to create a new branch of your copy of repository and then perform your work on it. This is called using a *feature* or *topic* branch. Feature branches are just branches of a repository where you perform work on only one thing—one feature—at a time. For instance, if you're working on an issue, you would create a branch just for fixing that issue. Once the issue is complete and the pull request has been accepted, it's no longer needed. You can delete the branch.

Here's an example of a new branch created for this chapter of the book:

```
Pliny:Book brasseur$ git checkout -b makeacontribution
Switched to a new branch 'makeacontribution'
```

Working in this way enables you to work on multiple features or topics at once without contaminating the work for one with the work for another. It allows for a very rigid separation of concerns that prevents committing unneeded or prototype work. It also allows for much easier updates should your pull request require some changes before it can be merged. Simply commit and push new changes to the pull request's feature branch, and they're automatically applied to the request. It's a tidy and efficient process.

While this is currently the most common approach to making a contribution to a FOSS project's repository, it's by no means the only one. Before you start your cloning-branching, always make sure to verify the process against the project's CONTRIBUTING file.

---

13. https://git-scm.com/book/en/v2/Git-Branching-Branches-in-a-Nutshell

Atomic Commits

OK, so *now* you can start working on your contribution. As you do so, make sure to follow the old adage: *Commit early; commit often.* Tightly scoped—also known as *atomic*—commits are safer commits. With an atomic commit, you easily can see what you've changed, because your commits are scoped to a single (usually small) topic, feature, or bug fix. This reduces the risk of contributing unnecessary changes. Atomic commits are also much easier to review afterward and to back out should something go wrong. When you make atomic commits, they affect and touch as little of the project as possible, therefore reducing the potential ripple effects of your changes.

Let's get metaphorical: Think of your complete contribution as an essay. It's composed of different paragraphs, each containing a complete thought, but each also requiring the context of the other paragraphs to meet the overall goal of the essay. An atomic commit is like a paragraph: it's a complete thought. Each time you finish a thought, commit it to the repository. If your contribution requires several different steps to complete (rename variables, pull duplicate code into a new function, call the new function in the correct locations), each step should be a separate, small commit. You may end up with several commits before your contribution is complete, but that's OK. It's much better to commit your work at the end of each thought than to risk losing all your work by waiting until the end of the contribution to save it to the repository. Some projects want you to use a *squash* or *rebase* feature in the version control software to consolidate all of those small commits into a single, larger atomic commit, so make sure to read the CONTRIBUTING file before submitting your contribution to the project.

Using Version Control for Non-Code Contributions

"But," you ask, "what if my contribution isn't code? Do I have to care about version control systems?"

A very good question! The answer, as you have probably already guessed, is "Yup."

Depending on the project, non-code contributions may not be maintained in the version control system (VCS). Documentation may be in a wiki, for instance. Designs may be in a shared drive system. It could be that you never have to use git, Subversion, Mercurial, or any of the other version control systems that are common across free and open source as well as proprietary software development.

However, considering how helpful it can be for any project to maintain all its related files in a single repository, it's likely that even if your contribution is not code, you'll still have to submit it to the VCS. Documentation, test plans, designs, and all other digital resources can be stored and shared using a version control system. You can even use one for your own personal writing or design projects. Doing so not only provides off-site backup of these important files, but it also kills off the Frankenstein's Monster file naming schemes, such as logo-new-FINAL-FINAL2-FINALwithedits-FINALapproved-OKreallydonenowhonest.ai. Instead of changing the file name, you simply commit it to the VCS. All previous versions are still there for you to access later if needed.

Even if the project does not use a version control system for non-code contributions, it's still helpful for you to learn about them. You are likely to find that the majority of community members for most projects are programmers. Learning the VCS terminology and how it is used builds empathy with the programmers, which will make it easier for you to communicate with the programmers in the project, and for you to understand the overall software development process. This is particularly helpful if your career path will have you working with programmers in the office.

So while it may not be necessary for you to learn the details of using a version control system for your own contributions, learning at least the basics will make you a more effective contributor and community member.

Test Your Contribution

As you're creating your contribution, make sure you test to confirm that it works at all (let alone does what you think it will). You might laugh, but a lot of highly skilled and experienced contributors have been tripped up by assuming their contribution will work only to learn after submitting it that the contribution is broken or totally wrong. Testing adds time up front but saves it later on. Testing should be continuous throughout the development of your contribution, but is especially important before you submit your contribution to the project.

Regardless of the type of contribution you're creating, test it against the appropriate version of the project to make sure it works as expected. If your contribution is code, provide both unit and integration tests as well as manually testing yourself. If your contribution is documentation or some other type, test how your change will appear in the official documentation repository, website, or wherever it may appear. No matter what, don't assume it's right. Even if it's just a small change, take the time to confirm not only that your change is correct, but also that you haven't accidentally jostled something else on your way.

Many projects have a continuous integration and deployment (CI/CD) service, such as Travis[14] or CircleCI.[15] This service runs all unit, integration, linter, and other tests on all submissions to confirm they meet project standards. If your selected project uses such a service, always pay attention to its results.

It is, by the way, completely OK if your contribution causes CI/CD to fail (*break the build*). This is actually very good news! Your contribution had a problem, but it hasn't been merged, so there's no harm done. You get the opportunity to fix your contribution and to improve in the process. You can learn a lot about a project by reviewing the different ways your contribution breaks the build.

To help others learn from your mistakes, consider documenting the build errors and the things that trigger them. This can be a great aid to new contributors who follow after you.

Diff Your Work

Before you submit your contribution, always do a diff on it. diff is a very old and very useful utility that's now built into most version control systems and IDEs. It simply shows you the differences between two files. In the case of version control, it typically shows you the differences between the files currently in your repository and the most recently committed versions of those files. It's also relatively easy to diff your repository or branch against other repositories, branches, or commits. This means you can see precisely how your branch differs from another branch (even one not on your computer), allowing you to confirm that your contribution will include only the changes necessary to complete your contribution.

You'll find some type of diff functionality in all version control systems and in most IDEs. Many operating systems also provide a diff utility. Check the documentation for your tools to see what options are available and how to use them.

Here's an example of what a diff looks like from the git version control system. In this diff, I changed a setting so the Glossary (included at the end of the book) would be included in the build:

---

14. https://travis-ci.org
15. https://circleci.com

```
Pliny:Book brasseur$ git diff ffcb48d e590486 jargon.pml
diff --git a/Book/jargon.pml b/Book/jargon.pml
index d0d452c..9a6ae33 100644
--- a/Book/jargon.pml
+++ b/Book/jargon.pml
@@ -1,6 +1,6 @@
 <?xml version="1.0" encoding="UTF-8"?>
 <!-- -*- markdown -*- -->
 <!DOCTYPE appendix SYSTEM "local/xml/markup.dtd">
-<appendix stubout="yes">
+<appendix stubout="no">
        <title>Glossary</title>
 <markdown>
```

It looks like there's a lot going on here, but once you get the hang of it, reading diffs can be pretty easy. I asked git to show me the differences between two versions of the file by using their commit hashes: git diff ffcb48d e590486. Because these commits included other files, and I only wanted to see the changes in the jargon file, I included its file name (jargon.pml) in the diff command. The diff returned a list of lines that changed between those two versions of the file. The line that was in the first version of the file (ffcb48d) but changed in the second (e590486) is prepended with a - character. The line that was changed or added in the second version of the file is prepended with a + character. Usually, unchanged lines are included on either side to help provide context.

There's obviously more happening in that diff, but these two +/- lines are the most important part. There are options you can pass to the diff command to make it display things differently,[16] but this is the gist of it and pretty much all you need to get started.

Submit Your Contribution

You may have crafted the Best Fix In The World, but it doesn't become a contribution until you actually submit it to the project. So how do you do that?

The contribution submission process is going to vary depending upon your contribution type (document, design, code, or another type) and the requirements and constraints of the project to which you've chosen to contribute.

Read the Docs

Each project will have a different preferred workflow for contributions, so remember to check the CONTRIBUTING file (see *Prepare to Contribute*) before trying to submit your contribution. This file probably contains some sort of directions

---

16. https://git-scm.com/docs/git-diff

for how to submit a contribution to the project. If it doesn't, ask the community for instructions or guidance. Once you've learned how the process works, share that knowledge with the community by updating the CONTRIBUTING file to help those who follow after you.

Lucky for you, you're looking to submit a contribution in a world where the git version control system is the most common way to contribute. BitBucket, GitLab, and especially GitHub are the reigning champions in the open source repository hosting world, each of them support git, and each of them make contributing a lot easier. While there are other hosting options, you'll find the overwhelming majority of projects on one of these services. This leads to a more or less standard set of processes for contributions, code, or otherwise. Isn't it nice to read that something is somewhat standardized, after all these pages of "every project does it differently"?

Introducing the Pull Request

The primary mechanism for submitting a contribution to these services is called a *pull request*. Some services call it a *merge request*, but this refers to more or less the same process. We'll use "pull request" or "PR" here, since these are what you'll hear people use most often.

The term "pull request" comes from the git commmand request-pull and was popularized in its current form by GitHub. In git, as a distributed version control system, each person can have their own copy of a repository, and each copy could be the source of other copies. One of these repositories is considered canonical. This repository often is called origin or master in the git documentation. To have a change in your version of the repository included in the canonical version, you make a *request* for the maintainers of origin to *pull* your changes into the canonical repository.

The pull request process is very well documented elsewhere,[17] therefore I won't go into it in detail, but I do think it's valuable to spend a few minutes giving you an overview. This will help you know what to expect when the time comes for you to submit your contribution.

Remember that diagram of the contribution process? No? That's OK, you can find it over on page 59. It'll be handy for you to refer back to it during the following explanation.

Starting from the origin in the upper left corner and working clockwise: you clone the repository, create your feature branch, and then make the changes

---

17. https://git-scm.com/docs/git-request-pull

necessary for your contribution. As you're working on your contribution, other people are continuing to submit and merge other changes into origin and evolving the project. Once you submit your pull request, you enter a feedback loop with community members, working with them to refine your contribution. After you've collaborated with them to put the final shine on it, a community member will pull (merge) your contribution into the project.

Make the Pull Request

Now you're ready to open that pull request to the origin repository. The actual steps for this vary by tool and by repository provider, so make sure to read their instructions before going forward. Whatever provider is used, the process will require some sort of a commit message. Chris Beams has an excellent article[18] detailing not only how to write a good commit message, but also why it's so important to do so. I recommend you read it, but I'll summarize some of the highlights here.

The individual steps may vary, but each process will ask for a description and some, for a title as well. Be descriptive. A title of "fixed stuff" with a blank description is not helpful to anyone. You want to make your pull request as easy as possible for the reviewer to understand. Titles should be brief (50 or so characters if you're using English) and should summarize the contents and intents of the contribution. Descriptions should be as detailed as necessary: don't skimp on words. Descriptions should include not only what you changed, but also why you changed it. If you're working on an issue, the description should reference that issue number. If you format the issue number with a hashtag at the front of it ("#42"), then many issue tracking systems will automatically link the issue with the pull request. This is very handy for contributor and reviewer alike.

An example of a pull request for the fixes on my book repository:

```
TITLE:
Add jargon file to the build

DESCRIPTION:
The jargon file has been commented out of the
build because we were in beta and doing a drip
of one chapter per beta release.

We've finally reached a point where all other
chapters are released, so it's time to include
the jargon file into the build so it can be
released as well.
```

---

18. https://chris.beams.io/posts/git-commit/

```
Flipped the stubout value accordingly.

Resolves issue #42
```

Before you actually submit your pull request, check the contributions guidelines one more time to make sure you're formatting and submitting your PR in the manner the project prefers. For instance, some projects prefer that you squash all of your commits for your contribution into a single commit.[19] Also, just to be completely sure you're only submitting changes required for this contribution, do one more diff of your work. This is especially important if you were working on multiple branches in your clone. Doing a diff before you send your pull request helps you confirm not only that you're sending the PR from the correct branch, but also that you're sending to the correct branch on the other side.

Patch: The Other Contribution Method

While the pull request process is the most common method for submitting a contribution to a free and open source project, it's not the only one. Free software came into being in 1983. Open source has existed since 1998. Git and the pull request process joined the world in 2005 and didn't become standard operating procedure until GitHub popularized it after the company was founded in 2008.

From 1983 until now, as you can imagine, there have been different processes for contributing to free and open source projects. At least one is in use today, so while I won't go into detail (abundant documentation is available on the internet), it's helpful for you to know about the other option that exists.

The predominant form of contributions prior to the invention of pull requests was *patch files*. A patch is a specialized diff that is dumped to a file and can then be shared to others and applied to a project. The process for creating and applying a patch file varies by version control system and by project. Because patch files were used extensively for so many years, you'll often hear people refer to all contributions as "patches," even if the contribution is submitted as a pull request.

While pull requests are the most common form of submission used today, some projects still rely on patch files for receiving contributions, including the Linux kernel. No matter which version control system your selected project uses (even if it's git), always review the project's contribution guidelines before assuming the submission process. Patch or pull request or passenger pigeon, always know the method for submitting a contribution before you get started.

---

19. https://git-scm.com/book/en/v2/Git-Tools-Rewriting-History

Review, Revise, Collaborate

Before your contribution is merged (pulled) into the origin repository, someone will review it to confirm that it does what you think it does, that it does something the project needs, and that it conforms to all project styleguides and standards. They probably will have questions, feedback, and suggestions about your contribution. Collaborate with them to get your contribution into an acceptable state. When you apply their feedback, use atomic commits to your feature branch. As you push these changes, they automatically appear on the pull request. This means you won't have to do anything special once you've applied all of the feedback and suggestions. Your contribution can simply be merged into the origin repository.

Congratulations! You've just made your first contribution! High fives all around!

Submit Work in Progress for Early Feedback

The process I just described implies that you should wait until your contribution is complete before sending a pull request to the project, but that's not always the case. Sometimes it can be very helpful to send a *work in progress* pull request while you're still creating your contribution. Just put WIP: at the start of your request title to let the reviewer know that you haven't finished the work quite yet. Also mention in the description that this is a work in progress and include any questions you have.

Why would you submit a pull request before your work is complete? For starters, doing so allows you to receive feedback early in the creation process. This can help you avoid going down some dark, thorny paths. Also, higher quality contributions come from receiving early feedback. The earlier and more often you receive feedback, the more likely it is that your contribution will be of a high quality. Finally, sending a work in progress pull request allows the project to see that someone is working on something, so they won't be surprised when a contribution appears in their pull request queue.

An example of a work in progress pull request:

```
TITLE:
WIP: Testing new section ordering

DESCRIPTION:
I've re-ordered the sections of this chapter in hopes
they'll flow better. WIP PR so Brian can have a look
and let me know what he thinks before I go much further
with the writing.

For issue #40
```

A Note on Feedback

This is a good time to pause and talk about feedback.

Not to put it too lightly, but feedback is great. Without feedback we keep making the same mistakes. Without feedback we can't learn and grow and evolve. It's one of the keys that makes free and open source collaboration work.

Unfortunately, most of us have a very hard time receiving feedback, let alone accepting it. We identify too closely with our contribution, such that criticisms of it—no matter how valid—are taken personally and put us on the defensive.

It doesn't help that most of us also have a hard time giving feedback, often delivering criticisms without empathy or in ways that are directed more at the person than at their contribution.

Both receiving and giving feedback are skills that can be learned and honed through practice. As you enter into this world of free and open source contributions, I encourage you to remember these tips:

- *You are not your contribution.* Even if the person providing the feedback is unskilled at it, and their criticisms come across as personally directed, try not to take their comments in that way. Try to focus on the aspects of their feedback that relate directly to your contribution, then guide the feedback conversation toward these elements.

- *It's not personal.* Problems found with your contribution are not problems found with you. You've put a lot of time and effort into that contribution, so naturally you feel a bit attached to it and that's OK. It's right to feel pride in what you've created and accomplished. But it's better to recognize that there's always a way to improve your contribution. Collaborate with those providing feedback to help evolve the contribution, the project, your knowledge, and your skills.

- *Feedback is a gift.* When people provide feedback on your contribution, they are freely sharing their knowledge and experience with you. You can use this feedback to grow into a more skilled contributor, then one day pay that gift forward as you provide feedback to others. This is part of the beneficial cycle that allows free and open source to grow.

- *Feedback and questions help make you better at what you do.* That's because feedback and questions help you see things you never have before and expand your mind and experiences in ways you never anticipated. None of us are perfect. None of us are all knowing. All of us have been in your position before: feeling excited at the newness but more than a little lost in it as well. It's OK. Ask questions. Ask for feedback. It's the only way not to feel lost, and we all want to help you.

- *If you get angry at some feedback, step away for a bit to cool off before responding.* It happens: a piece of feedback will get under your skin. Perhaps it was the way it was phrased. Maybe it's dismissing an implementation about which you have very strong opinions. Or maybe the person who gave the feedback is just an indelicate chowderhead. Like I said: it happens. Just because you're angry does not mean you have to react immediately. Replying in the heat of the moment rarely ends well for anyone involved. Take some time to cool off before responding. Go for a walk. Play with your pets or your kids. Spend some time on a hobby or other project. Fire up a good movie or video game. Whatever it takes, give yourself some space from the offending comment. Once you've had the time to cool off and think it over some more, then you can *respond* rather than *react.*

- *Always Assume Good Intent.* Above all, always assume good intent with all feedback. No matter how poorly a piece of feedback may be delivered, the person providing it is still giving you that gift of their knowledge and experience. They're not (usually) doing it to show off; they want the best for the project, for the contribution, and for you. Respect that and them and help them help you provide the best contribution you can. They mean well. Do you?

Tidy Up

Now that the project merged your contribution, you no longer need that feature branch that you created. It won't hurt anything if you leave it lying around, but it doesn't take long for these branches to build up and make a lot of clutter. Deleting it right after your pull request is accepted not only tidies up your testing environment, but it also makes it easier to locate the branches you need later and reduces the chance that you'll accidentally work on this now-dead branch. Removing a branch is quite easy from the command line. Here's an example where I removed a branch from my book repository:

```
Pliny:Book brasseur$ git branch -d makeacontribution
Deleted branch makeacontribution (was 74da8bc).
```

Note: This was a local branch. It's also possible to push a branch to the remote origin repository. An example of a command to delete a remote branch:

```
Pliny:Book brasseur$ git push origin --delete makeacontribution
```

Check the documentation for git for further instructions on branch use.[20]

Special Considerations for Windows-based Contributors

Is Microsoft Windows your jam? If so, you should know that you'll unfortunately have a much harder time contributing to most free and open source projects. Due to a couple of decades of Microsoft fear-mongering against open source, the majority of projects evolved such that they don't support Windows at all, not for building, contributing, nor using. While Microsoft has realized the error of its ways and embraced free and open source software, the FOSS legacy of not supporting Windows will take a lot longer to fade away. As you look at free and open source software projects, you'll find that most of them assume you're using a computer running Linux, one of the BSDs, or macOS. It's rare that a project has documented support for Windows and its users.

As a Windows user, you'll likely hit one or more of these common problems when you try to contribute:

- Installation and other scripts are written for shell/bash only.

- Path separators in scripts or the software itself assume Linux/BSD/macOS.

- Differences in the case sensitivities of file names (Linux: case-sensitive; Windows: case-insensitive). This is particularly a problem when using git.

- Windows defaults to a shorter maximum path length than Linux.

- Windows is rarely or poorly supported as a build platform.

- In general, the Windows development tooling is much different from Linux, the BSDs, or macOS.

- Merely being a Windows user or creating on Windows is seen as an imposition to the project.

With effort, you can overcome nearly all of these problems. Thankfully, Microsoft itself has done a lot of work lately specifically to support Windows users who wish to contribute to free and open source projects. Some of the solutions you may need are:

---

20. https://git-scm.com/book/en/v2/Git-Branching-Branches-in-a-Nutshell

- Use a cross-platform development tool such as Visual Studio Code.[21]

- Leverage the new tools available in the Windows Subsystem for Linux,[22] (WSL).

- Make sure you are using the latest Microsoft build tooling, which is c99/c++14 compliant.

- Use a virtual machine of a Linux or BSD variant.

- Use a container image of a Linux or BSD variant.

These things will help a lot with the technical hurdles to contributing, but what about the social? What if you come across one of those projects where merely being a Windows user makes you a second-class citizen? If all you have is Windows, and you meet resistance for your Windows-based contributions of any sort, there may not be much you can do. Those project maintainers have an operating system prejudice. You can try your best to convince them that your Windows-based contribution is a valuable addition to the project, but you may not be successful. Even if you are, you're unlikely to root out the technical prejudice ingrained in the project. Rather than deplete yourself by fighting a losing battle, consider thanking the project maintainers for their time and then finding a more welcoming and open-minded project and community.

There's More to Contributing Than Just Code

Choosing your contribution, triaging issues, creating and testing your work, submitting pull requests... Now you know exactly what to expect when you submit your first contribution to a free and open source project. Of course the details will vary a bit, but the overall picture will probably look a lot like what you've just read. It may seem like a lot, and you're right: it really is. Despite that, I know you'll get the hang of it. Your contributions may still take a lot of time—some contributions can be quite complex—but the process itself will become smooth. As with all other skills, all you need is practice.

While everyone who wants to participate in FOSS should be familiar with the contribution process in this chapter, it doesn't apply to all of the different types of contributions. What if, for example, you want to contribute but aren't a programmer? What types of contributions can a person make if they don't (or don't want to) code? The answer is: plenty, and the next chapter will detail a few of them.

---

21. https://code.visualstudio.com
22. https://blogs.msdn.microsoft.com/wsl/

CHAPTER 6

Make a Difference Without Making a Pull Request

When most people think of contributing to free and open source software projects, they usually think of the sort of thing we covered in the prior chapter: changing files to fix bugs or add features. These changes are then committed to the repository that holds the project's files. While this type of contribution certainly holds the greatest mindshare, it's far from the only way you can contribute to FOSS projects. It may not even be the most common type of contribution.

Some folks might tell you that programming or committing files is required for contributing to free and open source software projects, but you're smart enough to know that can't possibly be the case. A successful project requires many more types of contributions than writing code and documentation, designing user interfaces, providing translations, or any other type of contribution that requires committing files to the repository. All types of contributions are vital for the healthy growth and operation of a FOSS project and its community. Without help on non-committing contributions, the project would drown in administrative tasks, lack product direction, and be an unwelcoming space for community members. Those who supply non-commit contributions are the unsung heroes of the free and open source software world. If you're hoping to provide this type of contribution: Thank you! We in FOSS may not say it often enough, but we're grateful you're here.

So, what are these contributions that you can make without ever having to commit a file to the repository or to version control? I'm so glad you asked! There are a lot of different answers, but three of the most common are contribution review, contribution testing, and issue triage.

Review Contributions

Reviewing contributions is one way to contribute without committing a single file to version control, but it likely will require you to use version control to retrieve and view the contributions up for review.

We'll go through code reviews later in this chapter as a separate topic, but all types of contributions can benefit from another set of eyes on them. Reviewing a contribution helps locate defects early on in the process, when it's still relatively easy to fix them. It also helps to confirm that the work that was committed is actually the work that needs to be done. Very often either the issue is vague in describing the requirements or the contributor misunderstands them somehow. Catching these problems during review helps to get development back on track sooner.

Don't feel you have to be an expert in the contribution type to review the contribution. A less experienced designer can spot oversights in the work of someone who's been doing this for years. Everyone can read documentation to determine whether it flows well and provides answers users will need in a manner that makes sense. It doesn't take years of experience to test a contribution to make sure the feature or bug works as expected. Even new or amateur programmers can read a code contribution and ask why it was written a certain way. Never forget that asking questions during a review is a valuable way of revealing potential assumptions in any type of contribution.

For example, if you're reviewing API documentation, you might notice that the sample project referenced by some newly added sections is different from elsewhere in the documentation. It's possible that the other sample project didn't provide the functionality required to demonstrate what the author needed, but it's also possible that the author just didn't realize that the documentation was using a single sample project to help guide the reader through the process. Adding a comment to ask, "The rest of the doc uses a different sample project than this section. Is this intentional?" can help lead to clarifications in the documentation as well as in your understanding of it.

Reviews also are a wonderful way to learn a great deal about the project, its architecture, and its priorities. By reviewing the work of someone more experienced than you, you can see firsthand how they apply the best practices and knowledge they've gained through years of experience. Think of it as passive mentoring: you're learning from someone without them having to be there at all.

Aside from adding to your knowledge, reviewing is also a very important contribution to any project. While the final say in whether a contribution is accepted into the project repository typically lies in the hands of the core contributors, they often don't have the time to do the preliminary review and feedback of every single contribution. Having other (even new) contributors chip in on review can save core contributors a great deal of time. The first pass of reviewing is likely to catch a lot of the more obvious problems. If someone other than a core contributor can do that work, it frees the cores up for the more advanced reviews.

Please note, though: not all projects welcome contribution reviews from less experienced contributors. Before you invest a lot of time reviewing a contribution, check with the project community to verify that your help is needed.

No matter what type of contribution you review, do it in small chunks rather than in one big piece if at all possible. Atomic commits help with this, particularly for code or documentation contributions. Reviewing in the smaller segments provided by each atomic commit helps you to focus a little better and to take your time with the review rather than skimming it and moving on. Rushing through a contribution review misses not only potential bugs, but also the entire point of review: helping to ensure a quality contribution.

That doesn't mean that a contribution review should take forever though. If you're struggling with reviewing a contribution, and it feels like it's taking you more time than you think that type of review should, it's a sign that something might not be right. It could be that the contribution is more advanced than you're currently prepared to handle, or perhaps that you're getting mired in the minutiae like checking for consistency in variable naming schemes rather than whether the code makes sense. Or it could be that the contribution you're reviewing is unnecessarily complex and could use some refactoring to make it easier to understand and maintain in the future. Recognize when you might be spending too much time on a review and pause to ask another contributor whether they could have a look and give you a second opinion or help you understand what you're seeing.

As you're reviewing a contribution, you might feel tempted to point out some stylistic things that just aren't the way you would have done stuff. Here's how you handle those stylistic things: DON'T. If the contribution uses styles that violate the project's official styleguide, then definitely make a note of those, but otherwise try to stay away from stylistic comments. Your personal stylistic preferences don't matter here unless it's your contribution or your project, and even then, your preferences take a back seat to the styleguide, so stick to the styleguide for all stylistic review comments.

About Providing Feedback

We talked about receiving feedback in *Make a Contribution*. This is where we get to talk about the other side of that same coin: *providing* feedback.

If I tell you that something you did in your contribution is "stupid" or "naive," how would you feel? You'd probably be angry, hurt, or both, and rightfully so. These are mean-spirited words that when directed at people, can cut like knives. Words matter, and they matter a great deal. Therefore, put as much thought into the words you use when leaving feedback for a contribution as you do into any other form of contribution you give to the project. As you compose your feedback, think to yourself, "How would I feel if someone said this to me? Is there some way someone might take this another way, a less helpful way?" If the answer to that last question has even the chance of being a yes, backtrack and rewrite your feedback. It's better to spend a little time rewriting now than to spend a lot of time apologizing later.

When someone does make a mistake that seems like it should have been obvious, remember that we all have different experiences and knowledge. What's obvious to you may not be to someone else. And, if you recall, there once was a time when that thing was not obvious to you. We all make mistakes. We all typo. We all forget commas, semicolons, and closing brackets. Save yourself a lot of time and effort: point out the mistake, but leave out the judgement. Stick to the facts. After all, if the mistake is that obvious, then no critique will be necessary, right?

Remember to review only the contribution and not the person who contributed it. That is to say, point out, "*the contribution* could be more efficient here in this way..." rather than, "*you* did this inefficiently." The latter is *ad hominem* feedback. *Ad hominem* is a Latin phrase meaning "to the person," which is where your feedback is being directed: to the person who contributed it rather than to the contribution itself. By providing feedback on the person you make that feedback personal, and the contributor is justified in taking it personally. Be very careful when crafting your feedback to make sure you're addressing only the contents of the contribution and not accidentally criticizing the person who submitted it for review.

Not all of your feedback has to (or should) be critical. As you review the contribution and you see something that you like, provide feedback on that as well. Several academic studies—including an important one by *Baumeister, Braslavsky, Finkenauer, and Vohs [BBFV01]*—show that humans focus more on negative feedback than positive. When your feedback is solely negative, it can be very disheartening for contributors. Including positive reinforcement and feedback is very motivating to people and helps them feel good about their contribution and the time they spent on it, which all adds up to them feeling more inclined to provide another contribution in the future. It doesn't have to be some gushing paragraph of flowery praise, but a quick, "Huh, that's a really smart way to handle that. It makes everything flow really well," can go a long way toward encouraging someone to keep contributing.

Praise is one less common but valuable type of review feedback. Questions are another. If you're looking at a contribution and can't tell why the submitter did things the way they did, or if the contribution just doesn't make a lot of sense to you, asking for more information acts as feedback. It tells the submitter that something they contributed isn't as clear as they thought and that it may need some work to make the approach more obvious, or if it's a code contribution, a comment to explain what's going on and why. A simple, "I don't understand this part here. Could you please tell me what it's doing and why you chose that way?" can start a dialogue that leads to a contribution that's much easier for future contributors to understand and maintain.

Using questions as a form of feedback implies that there will be answers to those questions...or perhaps other questions in response. Whether your feedback is in question or statement format, you should expect to generate some sort of dialogue throughout the process. An alternative is to see your feedback as incontrovertible, your word as law. While this is definitely one approach you can take, it's rarely a good one. When providing feedback on a contribution, it's best to collaborate rather than dictate. As these dialogues arise, it's important to embrace them as opportunities for conversation and learning on both sides. Be willing to discuss their approach and your feedback, and to take the time to understand their perspective.

The bottom line is: Don't be a jerk. If you're not sure whether the feedback you're planning to leave makes you sound like a jerk, pause to have someone else review it before you click Send. Have empathy for the person at the receiving end of that feedback. While the maxim is thousands of years old, it still rings true today that you should try to do unto others as you would have them do unto you. Put yourself in their shoes and aim to be helpful and supportive rather than simply being right.

Code Review

Even new programmers can provide a lot of value with their code reviews. You don't have to be a Rockstar Ninja 10x Unicorn Diva programmer with years and years of experience to have valuable insights. In fact, you don't even have to be a programmer at all. You just have to be knowledgable enough to spot patterns. While you won't be able to do a complete review without programming knowledge, you may still spot things that could use some work or clarification.

If you're not a Rockstar Ninja 10x Unicorn Diva programmer, not only is your code review feedback still valuable, but you can also learn a great deal in the process: Code layout, programming style, domain knowledge, best practices, neat little programming tricks you'd not have seen otherwise, and sometimes *antipatterns* (or "how not to do things"). So don't let the fact that you're unfamiliar with the code, the project, or the language hold you back from reviewing code contributions. Give it a go and see what there is to learn and discover.

"But," you may wail, "how is that even possible?! I don't know how to program very well! How could I ever do anything valuable on a code review?" Calm yourself, friend. You have a lot to offer here. Earlier I mentioned pattern-spotting, and that's a good place to start. If the contribution you're reviewing looks a lot more complicated than everything around it, you've just spotted a potential problem. Does the code use different indentations or variable naming than elsewhere in the file? That's another potential problem. Is the code contribution really long, when everything else in the file is much shorter? That could be a sign something is wrong. You don't have to be that Rockstar Ninja 10x Unicorn Diva programmer to spot these things; you only have to be familiar with programming and—most importantly—you only have to be looking at the code.

Do be careful as you start code review for a project with which you're not very familiar. Some projects would rather not receive reviews from people who aren't yet skilled in the code in question, as those reviews often can contain errors or inconsistencies with how the project typically operates. Inexperienced reviewers also can confuse inexperienced contributors, who might not know that the person providing feedback to them is not very familiar with the code or the project. Always check the CONTRIBUTING file or ask a core contributor before you start reviewing code contributions, rather than risk stepping on toes or providing feedback when none is wanted.

What to Look for in a Code Review

If you do decide to review code contributions, what kind of things should you look for? The answer, as you probably expect, is "it depends on the project." That said, there are several things you can keep in mind regardless of the project, the code, or the programming language being used. While it may seem like these tips are only for people earlier in their programming career, nothing could be further from the truth. What follows are best practices for code reviews by people of any experience level. Whether you're a neophyte or a master, these tips can help you spot potential problems in any code review.

- *Does the code even pass the build?* Does the project use continuous integration/continuous deployment (CI/CD) or otherwise have its test suite run automatically? If the test suite doesn't pass after the code contribution... You're a smart person. I don't need to tell you that this is a big red flag that something may be wrong with that code. Politely ask the contributor to study the build/test errors and correct them before you continue to invest your time in reviewing the contribution.

- *Is the code even readable?* You don't have to be an expert in a programming language to tell whether the code is readable. Strange loops, short and vague variable and function names, inconsistent use of whitespace or brackets, large blocks of commented out code... Many things could make a piece of code difficult to read, but the end result is the same: unreadable code is unmaintainable code.

- *Do one thing and do it well.* It's best practice that each class, method, or function in a program do one thing and do it well. This reduces the complexity of any one piece of code, making it shorter and much easier to understand, maintain, and test. Be on the lookout for any piece of code that's overloaded and trying to do too many things. A good clue for this can be that the code has a complicated or long conditional statement.

- *The DRY Principle: Don't Repeat Yourself.* Is there any code that occurs more than once, even if it's doing similar but not entirely identical things? If so, it should be refactored out into a separate class, method, or function. Repeated code means changes have to be applied in multiple places, leading to a higher chance of error. Plus, refactoring it out can make it easier to test.

- *How is the error handling?* Are errors explicitly handled? Are they even handled at all? Do errors include descriptive messages or are they vague, "an error has occurred"-type things? Proper error handling doesn't only make debugging a lot easier; it improves the experience for everyone who uses the program.

- *Is the code efficient?* More advanced programmers will have an easier time of determining this for a new piece of code, but even new programmers can have a feeling for whether code appears unwieldy, or whether it looks like it's working harder than it should to accomplish what it does. If your instinct tells you that the code may not be efficient, it may be worth flagging for more explanation.

- *How is the test coverage?* Does the code come with any tests? Both unit and integration? If the code was covered by existing tests, were they updated to make sure they're still valid? If it's new code or there were no tests before, did the author add any? If there are tests, don't forget to review those as well as the rest of the code.

- *Does the code actually do what it's supposed to?* If the code is intended to add a feature or fix a bug, compare the code against the issue it's supposed to close to make sure the code does what's expected of it. It's very easy to misunderstand expected functionality, forget to include a piece, or include more than is expected (more is not always better).

- *Is the code documented?* Code comments, installation instructions, user docs, API docs, troubleshooting docs... There are so many different ways a piece of code could or should be documented. Because documentation is so difficult, yet so important, it's usually easier to do it piecemeal as each new feature or bug fix is added to the repository. If the code you're reviewing doesn't come with changes to the documentation, you may want to suggest the author add some to help avoid the technical and usability debt that can accrue by skipping documentation.

As you can see, while knowing about code is very helpful when doing code review, there are a lot of things you can see and provide feedback on even if you're just getting started with programming. If the project is supportive of it, even less experienced programmers can provide a lot of valuable insights while also learning more about the project code and how it all fits together.

Provide Testing

Testing is a great way to contribute to a project without writing a single line of code. Providing a bit of testing kicks off a beneficial cycle. The more testing a contribution receives, the more problems are spotted earlier in the process. The more problems are spotted, the higher the quality and therefore also the higher the reputation of the project. Projects with great reputations attract more users and from there, also more contributors, and the testing and quality cycle begins all over again.

When I say "testing," I don't mean writing unit or integration tests (though those are certainly welcome, too). As I mentioned earlier, all types of contributions can benefit from having another set of eyes on them, and testing provides those eyes. Documentation, design, interfaces, bugs, features, usability, accessibility:

These things and many more need review and testing to make sure they work as expected and provide value to the end user.

Test the Docs

One project element that's relatively easy to test but even easier to overlook is the documentation. So often we fire off a little piece of docs with our contributions but don't take the time to confirm that the docs are accurate, make sense, flow well, or even describe what we think they're describing. More often we don't write docs at all, so the people who follow after us are left scratching their heads wondering whether a feature exists, and if it does, how to use it. Documentation testing includes looking for things like:

- Does the documentation exist at all? If it doesn't, should it? (Hint: the answer is probably yes.)

- Is it readable? Or does the grammar, spelling, and organization need some work?

- Is it consistent, or does the style and organization change from author to author?

- Relatedly, if there is a documentation style guide, does the documentation follow it?

- Is it useful for the target audience? Will it allow them to accomplish their goals?

- Is it comprehensive? Does it cover all of the questions a reader may have?

These items are about the content of the documentation, but the structure is important as well. For instance, do all of the links work and do they go to the sites or other documents that they should? Should there be more or fewer links? If there are images, do they display well? How does the documentation look on different devices or in different browsers? Each one of these can have a big effect on the effectiveness and the usability of the project.

Test the Interfaces

Documentation is only one aspect of the usability of a project. As you can imagine, several others also need attention and testing if the project wants to be easy for people to use. Interfaces—command line, graphical, and programming—all need people to review them and make sure they're consistent and logical. All interface actions should include user feedback so people know that something is happening. If it's a graphical interface, the purpose of all the elements should be clear, even if that requires explanatory text in tooltips.

Whatever the interface, it should meet the user where they are, taking advantage of common interface idioms rather than creating novel, unexpected, and undocumented ways to interact with the software. By testing for and revealing usability issues, you can help the project become more friendly for new people to try, increasing its user (and potential contributor) base.

Test the Accessibility

A specialized and unfortunately easily overlooked aspect of usability is the accessibility of the project, that is, ensuring it's designed and programmed in such a way as to provide access to as many different people as possible, including those with disabilities. While a bit harder to test on the command line side of things, there are several standard accessibility tests that you can perform on graphical interfaces:

- All images have descriptive alt attributes.

- All form elements have associated and descriptive label elements.

- When you turn the contrast on your monitor all the way down (a very rough simulation of color blindness), the interface is still readable and usable.

- When you increase the font size, the interface is still readable and usable.

There are many other interface elements you can test for accessibility. The WebAIM[1] project maintains resources and a handy list[2] to help you learn more about web accessibility.

If you have experience or an interest in information security, you'll find that your skills are in demand in FOSS projects. More experienced security specialists will be able to review project code to determine whether it leaks or exposes sensitive information or whether it performs adequate validation on all inputs. Less experienced security enthusiasts can be very helpful by performing manual input validation tests, or even automated fuzz testing, to test for vulnerabilities in the project's interfaces.

While these are the most common types of testing you may come across in FOSS projects, it's still not a complete list. As you navigate, contribute to, and participate in the community for your free and open source project, be on the lookout for other ways where you could add another pair of eyes to help ensure the quality of the project and a good experience for those who use and contribute to it.

---

1.   https://webaim.org
2.   https://webaim.org/resources/evalquickref/

Triage Issues

We talked a bit about issue triage back in *Make a Contribution*, but that was in the context of an issue or feature you wanted to work on yourself. While this is useful, you don't have to be the one to fix the bug to be the one to test whether it's actually a problem. Bugs and feature requests come in all the time for FOSS projects, and it can be helpful to have people reviewing them as they come in, exposing the signal amidst the issue noise. While some projects prefer that more experienced contributors triage issues, others are thrilled to have less experienced people lend a hand as the first responders to any new issues that arrive.

Before you start triaging issues, take a moment to confirm not only that the project welcomes this type of contribution from people of your skill level (whatever that may be) but also how they prefer triaging be handled. One of the reasons projects avoid having less experienced people triage their issues is that those folks aren't as familiar with the project's issue tags, severities, priorities, or workflow. For instance, in some projects *issue triage* includes defining each issue's severity and its priority on the roadmap. Less experienced contributors often lack the big picture view necessary to make these severity and priority determinations, so some projects prefer that only very experienced contributors perform triage. Mis-tagged issues can cause a delay in fixing issues and require a lot of time to clean up, so some projects avoid this by limiting the people who may triage and tag issues. Check to see whether your project is one of those before you spend a lot of time trying to duplicate a newly reported bug. As always, if a project has guidelines or documentation for bug triage, read and obey these guidelines.

While you probably won't need to commit any changes to the repository to triage issues as they come in, you will almost assuredly need to have a testing/development environment set up, if not also need to be running a local copy of the project. This can take a fair amount of time to prepare, and will require maintenance to keep up to date. If you're already contributing changes to the repository, this setup and maintenance time may not be that big of a deal. If you're not, be prepared to invest time in this. Triaging and testing issues against an out-of-date setup or install only wastes your time.

Don't Forget to Read First

The first step of any issue triage is to read through the issue. Yes, I know: groundbreaking revelation, right? In all seriousness, though, you'd be surprised at how many people dive in attempting to duplicate an issue before they fully understand what it is that the issue is trying to describe. This can lead to a lot of frustration and wasted time on all sides, but is relatively easy to avoid simply by taking a "read first, understand second, act third" approach.

As you're reading through the issue, if it appears to be reporting or is at all concerned with a matter of privacy or security, *escalate it immediately*. Security should never be taken lightly, and it's always far better to be safe rather than sorry where information security (*infosec*) is involved. Even if you're a seasoned infosec specialist, always notify the core project developers that there may be a security problem. This is not the sort of thing you want to surprise people with at the last moment. Notify the team and allow them to prepare to fix the issue, should it prove to be a legitimate concern.

Tips for Triage

While the actual steps for triage will vary from bug to bug and issue to issue, the following guidelines can apply to nearly every issue you look at.

- *Does the issue even make sense?* Be it a difference in perspective, under-standing, or language, sometimes an issue will arrive and you simply can't comprehend what the reporter is trying to say. That's OK; communication problems happen. Reply back asking for a clarification. It can help to guide the conversation with a statment such as, "I think you mean... Do I have that right?"

- *Do you understand the issue?* Can you tell what the problem is, or is more information required? If the latter, politely request it from the person who filed the issue.

- *Is it formatted correctly?* Many projects have an issue template or provide issue-creation guidance in their CONTRIBUTING file. If your project does this, check to make sure the person who opened the issue followed the template or guidance. If they haven't, politely direct them to the instructions and ask for corrections to the issue they filed.

- *Is the issue for a platform the project supports?* Some projects don't work (or aren't supported) on all platforms. If the person who wrote the issue doesn't mention platform, politely ask for it. If the platform is mentioned but is one the project doesn't support, close the issue with a polite note explaining the reason.

- *Is the reporter using the latest version of the project?* If the reporter doesn't mention the version of the project they're using, politely reply back and ask for this information. It can be difficult to troubleshoot issues that are made against older versions of the project. It's also possible that the reporter's issue is resolved in more recent versions. If the project doesn't explicitly state that it supports older versions, politely ask the issue reporter to upgrate to the latest version of the project and try to duplicate what they reported.

- *Is the issue a duplicate?* Search the issue tracker (for both open and closed issues) to see whether this issue has been reported before. If it has, politely close the issue as a duplicate. Some projects track duplicates through tagging and/or cross-referencing, so be sure to follow the correct procedure for your project.

- *What category is the issue?* Is it a bug? A support request? A feature request? Noise/spam? Tag the issue accordingly to make it easier to find in the future (or close the issue if it's just spam).

- *Are there steps to duplicate the problem?* If the issue is reporting a bug or a problem with the project, has the reporter included steps for how to reproduce the problem? If not, politely reply asking them to provide these steps.

- *Can you reproduce the problem?* If the issue is reporting a problem, can you reproduce it? If so, add a note to the issue including the steps that you used to reproduce it and anything new you learned in the process. If you can't reproduce the problem, it may be that you don't know enough to duplicate it. That's perfectly OK. Make a note that you can't reproduce the problem, then either politely ask someone for help or move on to triaging another issue.

While these tips are for triaging issues you don't intend to work on, they apply just as well to those you do. So if during your triage you find that you'd like to fix an issue that you're looking at, don't hesitate to follow your project's steps and guidelines for contribution.

Volunteer for the Less Interesting Things

Every project has tedious tasks that need to be done but no one really enjoys doing: data entry, data cleanup, small repetitive tasks, things like that. These are activities that don't seem like a big deal but add up quickly...in good ways when the activities are completed, in bad ways when they're neglected.

Tasks like these are excellent for people who are new to a FOSS project. As a new contributor, taking on this sort of task enables you to learn a lot about how the project is organized and operates, which can help when you're making other types of contributions. More importantly, tasks like these make a big difference to the community. They may be small and less interesting, but they're valuable. When a newer contributor takes on these tasks, it frees up experienced contributors to tackle the more advanced duties of maintaining a free and open source project. Volunteering for the grunt work demonstrates that you, as a new contributor, are willing to commit to the community as a whole, rather than simply to the project, which does wonders for your reputation within that community. If you're willing to help in this way, people will be much more willing to help you in return later.

This sort of less interesting task isn't usually written up in the issue tracker, so how can you, enterprising new contributor, locate them? There are two ways to go about this: the passive way and the active way. For the passive way, you simply pay a lot of attention to the various communication media for the project (usually real-time chat and mailing list). As you see a less interesting task mentioned, raise your hand and volunteer to help with it. For the active way, you don't wait to see a less interesting task mentioned before raising your hand to volunteer. Instead, ask people directly whether there's anything with which you could help. A quick question of, "Hey, I'm new here and would love to help out with some of the tedious administrative things while I learn. Where should I start?" can do wonders for turning up the less interesting tasks that the more experienced contributors would rather off-load to someone else.

There Are So Many Options

By now you've probably figured out that, yes, it's not only possible to contribute to a free and open source project without ever having to write a line of code or submitting a single file to version control, but often these types of contributions can also be some of the most important. Plenty of people *commit* to the community without a *commit* to version control, and their contributions are priceless. The types of contributions in this chapter aren't a complete list, of course, and naturally each project will have different requirements and needs—for instance, project management, translation, marketing, advocacy, and customer support are some of the many ways to contribute to a FOSS project without committing a single file to the repository. Always be on the lookout for the ways you might lend a hand to the project, and you'll be surprised at the diverse ways you can help and join the community.

CHAPTER 7

Interact with the Community

You've overcome all the roadblocks in your way, you've followed all instructions to the letter, and you've finally submitted your first contribution.

Congratulations!

In free and open source software, the only feeling more amazing than making your first contribution is having it accepted as part of the project. When and how does that happen? You probably won't be surprised to hear the answer is, "It Depends." It'll depend on the project itself, your contribution, whether anyone is available to review your contribution, and any number of other vague and mysterious variables.

After Your First Contribution

Once you submit your contribution, you must practice this little thing we like to call Patience. There are any number of reasons that it might take a while for the project members to get around to reviewing your contribution. Sometimes you'll find a project that has a policy to try to review any contribution within a certain amount of time, but few projects have the available people power to make a promise like that. Your contribution will have to wait in line with all the rest of them, until someone is available to have a look at it. If someone hasn't reviewed your contribution in a couple of weeks, feel free to drop a gentle question into the project community's preferred communication route asking when you can expect someone to review it. And while you should not need a reminder, always be polite.

After someone has the chance to review your contribution, they will undoubtedly have some feedback for you. I covered feedback in *Make a Contribution*, so I won't tread that ground again. However, it's worth reiterating that if you receive feedback you don't understand, you should ask for clarification rather than simply ignore it. Someone took the time to review your contribution and provide feedback, but that doesn't necessarily mean that the person is good at writing feedback. They may assume you have knowledge or experience you don't have, or it could be that their primary language is not the one in which they wrote the feedback. Asking, "I'm not sure I understand. Do you mean that I should do *this thing* instead?" can go a long way in making sure your contribution is successful.

Sometimes Your Contribution Is Not Accepted

No matter how good and worthwhile you think your contribution is, it's possible that the project maintainers will not accept it. Don't take this personally, as it's certainly not intended that way. There are plenty of reasons your contribution may not be accepted:

- *You've provided something the project simply does not need.* You can avoid this problem by working on only existing bugs or issues, or by writing up an issue for your idea and discussing it with the project maintainers before you spend a lot of time crafting your contribution.

- *Your contribution is a duplicate of someone else's.* Once in a while, you'll have the same great idea as someone else, but they either beat you to it or provide an implementation that the project maintainers prefer. If you discuss your contribution idea with the maintainers before diving in, you usually can learn whether someone else is already working on something similar. If so, you can collaborate with that person and contribute it together. You can learn a lot this way.

- *Your contribution did not follow project guidelines.* Perhaps you didn't follow the styleguide, you didn't submit it in the format desired, or you otherwise made a mistake with your contribution. This could be a sign of poor project documentation...or that you simply didn't read the documentation.

No matter the reason, if the maintainers don't accept your contribution, you should ask how you could improve so that your next contribution has a better chance of being successful. Solicit feedback and take it to heart. That's the best way to improve.

What to Do While Waiting for a Review

While you're waiting for someone to review your contribution, there's no reason to sit there idle. Did you learn anything during the contribution process? For instance, did you overcome a problem during installation, discover a new error condition, or find that the API documentation wasn't as clear as you hoped? Documenting those findings is a very valuable contribution, and right after a contribution, while everything is still fresh in your mind, is the perfect time to capture that knowledge and contribute it back to the community. Did you find something during your contribution that you think could work more smoothly? If you don't have the time to fix or add the documentation yourself, write it up in the project's issue tracker, so there's a good chance of someone else adding it to the docs later.

But Usually: It's Accepted! (Eventually)

Sure, rejection is possible. However, while it may take a few rounds of review and revision, most of the time, your contribution will be accepted by the project maintainers. In FOSS jargon, this is called *landing your first patch*, and it feels great. Now that it's accepted though, what do you do next?

The most obvious answer is: start working on your next contribution. Even if you're still waiting for your first patch to land, there's no reason that you can't locate and work on another issue for the project. A tried but true approach to finding a new contribution is to just ask. "While I'm waiting for my patch to merge, does anyone need help with anything?" is a wonderful way to signal to the community that you're not only available to help, but most importantly are willing to do so. Don't wait for someone to signal they'd like a hand; offer one yourself.

I caution you not to work on too many different issues at once if you can help it, but starting a new one while you're waiting to close out the first is perfectly reasonable. Also reasonable is moving on to another project. It's possible that the contribution you submitted is the only one you wanted to make. This often is the case when you're contributing for a work project and just need to get this one fix into the FOSS project, so you can keep making progress on your work project that uses it. There's nothing wrong with this and no obligation to stick around in the community. Naturally it's very nice if you do stick around, but everyone understands that you have other things going on in your life, so usually they don't mind if you make one contribution and then move on.

Once your contribution is accepted—your patch lands—it's part of the project and usually is no longer your responsibility. You're not required to maintain it if you don't want or aren't able; the entire community is now there to help keep it up to date and healthy. As the person who created it, and therefore, the domain specialist for that piece, you may naturally be called upon to answer questions, but it's rare that anyone expects you to be the sole maintainer of that one piece of the project from there on out. You can feel free to move on to working on something else.

Get Help

As you're chipping away at your contribution, you'll probably hit a few snags and will need assistance to continue. Sometimes you have the resources available to help yourself, and nearly every free and open source project assumes that you'll try this avenue first before asking someone for assistance. In the tech industry, this is known as *RTFM*: Read The F'ing Manual. I'll leave it to you to choose which word to use for the *F*.

RTFM

The manual in question is generally defined as any sort of documentation that the project makes available. This could be user docs, installation docs, developer docs, the contributing guide, styleguides, or any number of other types of documentation. You may find that most documentation in free and open source projects needs a lot of work to be as useful as you'd like. It takes a lot of time and effort to develop documentation, so unfortunately, it's often overlooked by the project developers. Even if your project of choice is very sparsely documented, take the time to read the docs that *do* exist before asking for assistance. If nothing else, the docs will provide more context so you can better understand not only the answer you'll receive, but also how to ask your question more effectively in the first place.

Another great place to look for information about any problems you have is the project's communication archive. If the project has a mailing list, it will be particularly helpful. Nearly every mailing list archive is both viewable and searchable online, which makes researching your problem much easier. Often the hardest part is locating the archives at all. If you subscribed to the mailing list, you'll often find a link to the archive in the footer of messages you received. If you don't see it there, dig up the confirmation email you received when you subscribed. That typically includes a link to the interface where you can maintain your subscription and usually also includes a way to view the list archives. If the project uses real-time chat (IRC, for instance), it may log and archive conversations from the chat system. If these logs exist, they will be either linked in the topic or subject of the chat system or documented some-where. Searching all of these archives may lead to the answer to your problem.

You can also learn a lot from past contributions to the project. If you have a local clone of the project's repository, you can use the version control system to search the past commits. If the project uses a forge like GitLab, GitHub, or BitBucket, it can be very easy to search all past commit logs as well as closed issues (sometimes all at once). These searches can turn up valuable information about previous problems people have faced and point you toward potential fixes.

How to Ask a Question

If after all of your reading and searching, you still haven't overcome your roadblock, don't hesitate to ask the community for help. Asking, however, should be done properly. No matter how frustrated you may feel, don't blurt out an irritated question in the chatroom or on the mailing list. If you come across as unfriendly, you can expect to receive very little help. No one wants to donate their time to help a grump. There are five steps to asking a good question of a free and open source project community:

1. *Verify you're asking in the appropriate venue.* Some projects want you to ask on the mailing list. Others in the issue tracker. Still others in the chatroom or by some other mechanism. Make sure to review the CONTRIBUTING file to verify the correct way to ask questions for that project.

2. *Drop the attitude.* Even if you've contributed to other projects before, even if you've been in software development for thirty years, even if you're Linus Torvalds[1], Larry Wall[2], and Tim Berners-Lee[3] all rolled into one: Get over yourself. It's entirely possible to phrase a question that is confident and competent yet does not make you sound like an arrogant twit. For instance, when asking about a programming optimization, rather than pointing out that you have a PhD in computer science and have been programming in that language for twelve years (information which is irrelevant to the suggestion at hand), simply state the problem you've noticed, how the code could be improved, and ask whether anyone would have a problem with you making the change. Take the time to craft your question accordingly. Run a draft past a friend just to be sure you don't come across as a conceited jerk.

3. *Always be polite.* Again, no matter how frustrated you may feel, be polite when asking your question of the community. It's OK to let your exasperation come through, as long as you don't direct it toward the project or the community. "I've read all the docs and the mailing list and tried everything I could think of, but it still doesn't work," is an entirely acceptable statement. "These docs are useless, the code is a mess, and the error messages are horrible," is a statement that—no matter how true it may be—is unlikely to

---

1. https://en.wikipedia.org/wiki/Linus_Torvalds; The inventor of Linux.
2. https://en.wikipedia.org/wiki/Larry_Wall; The inventor of rn, patch, Perl, and Perl 6.
3. https://en.wikipedia.org/wiki/Tim_Berners-Lee; The inventor of the World Wide Web.

win you any friends. Say please and thank you and make sure that your words express only the problem and not any directed negativity.

4. *Succinctly but clearly state your problem.* State what you are trying to accomplish, what you are experiencing instead, and the full text of any error messages you see. Be brief, but make sure to include all relevant details. If you have a log file or stack trace, drop it into a pastebin[4] or similar service, then provide a link to it in your question. It can be helpful to summarize the steps you took to troubleshoot the problem, as well as any research you've done. This will allow people to suggest new solutions rather than those you've already tried.

5. *Be patient.* Remember: nearly every member of a free and open source software community is a volunteer. Each will have their own life and all of the complexities that accompany it. Give them a few days to reply to your question before you ping to ask whether anyone saw it. While you're waiting, you could help the entire community by documenting anything you learned in your research while troubleshooting your problem (such as error messages and what they mean).

General Tips for Participating in Discussions

Across all of the FOSS contribution process, communication is probably where the most unwritten rules hide. Over the decades, the free and open source software world has developed a lot of habits and expectations about how to communicate. Naturally, as with all other aspects of contributing, these habits and expectations vary from community to community. By now, it probably won't surprise you that however much these things vary, there are still some guidelines that apply to most situations.

We'll get into guidelines for specific types of communication channels in a moment, but first, there are some guidelines that apply across all forms of communication. Practicing these will help your communications be much more effective.

*   *Listen and read more than you speak and write*: A civil discussion can quickly turn heated through simple misunderstandings. Often these misunderstandings come from not taking in all of the information being presented to us. You may reply having only seen part of the whole picture, and your reply can spark flames. Take the time to read or listen to the complete set of information before you reply.

---

4. https://en.wikipedia.org/wiki/Pastebin

- *Comprehend, then act rather than react*: There's a difference between listening and hearing. When reviewing a discussion, pause to make sure you absorb it. Listen to what the other participants are trying to say; don't simply hear their words. If you have a strong emotional reaction, either positive or negative, try to wait a bit before responding. Think your response through, including the impact that it may have on the others in the discussion. Knee-jerk reactions are rarely an effective way to collaborate with others.

- *Try to understand other perspectives (ask for more information if you don't)*: As you're working to comprehend the technical aspects of the discussion, take the time to consider the perspectives of the other people participating. Free and open source software is populated by brilliant people just like you, and those people rarely do anything without what they believe is a good reason (even if you don't agree with it). If you don't understand the perspective or reason for a suggestion, ask. A simple, "I think you're suggesting *this thing*, but I'm still not clear on your reasoning. Could you please give me more information?" can avoid miscommunication and flaring tempers.

- *It's not a competition*: No one is keeping score in these discussions. There is no race to be the first one to have a suggestion accepted. A dialogue is not a competition, and there's no reason to treat it as one. If you're usually a very competitive type of person, keep that in mind while participating in the discussion and be very aware of your responses. Who are you trying to benefit with them? Are you working for the good of the project, or are you trying to "win" the discussion? Be honest with yourself, and try to craft your responses to help the project rather than draw attention or praise to yourself.

- *It's not about you*: Relatedly, it's going to be pretty rare that a discussion in a free and open source project is about you, but if it is, then it's possible something may have gone hideously awry. Aside from those rare occasions, these discussions are not personally directed and should be about matters that concern the project. If your suggestions or questions are not accepted during the discussion, it's not an attack against your skills or worth as a human or as a contributor. It's simply that the suggestions or questions are not accepted; don't take it personally. If it turns out that it is an actual attack against your skills or worth as a human...well, we'll cover that in the next chapter.

- *Keep it public*: Above all, remember: these are public projects with distributed communities, perhaps globally so. Conversations related to the project should occur in the public space, be it issue tracker, mailing list, real-time chat, or in person. If sometimes a smaller group needs to split off to discuss a specific topic, the results of that discussion should be reported to the entire community in some way. While there are exceptions (discussions about Code of Conduct violation reports, for instance), private discussions and decisions have little place in a FOSS community or project.

Keep these guidelines in mind whenever you're participating in discussions in free and open source communities. By using these tips, you'll exhibit respect for the community and its members and gain a lot of respect yourself. As a respected member of the community, your contributions will gain in their effectiveness and impact, all because you took the time to learn how to communicate well.

The Importance of Setting Up and Maintaining Expectations

Many of the communication problems that any group of people face come from not paying attention to the expectations we have or we create in the minds of others. As we share our words and thoughts, those who experience them construct a series of assumptions and expectations based upon our words. When the actions we take end up not meeting the expectations someone else holds, disappointment usually follows.

When working on a contribution, the best way to avoid disappointment is to take the expectation setting into your own hands. You can do this by being very clear about what you will do in your contribution, why, and by when. Think of this as the communication version of the *Principle of Least Astonishment*, commonly used in user interface design. If you take actions that are expected, no one will be surprised (or disappointed).

When setting up contribution expectations, you can't always be sure that those expectations are actually seen or understood by the other participants of the discussion. Assuming that everyone took the same information away from a conversation is a good way to set yourself up for failure and arguments. As it's unlikely you're a mind reader, how can you tell whether the entire group now shares the same set of expectations? You ask. For instance: "OK, just to verify, I'm going to remove that feature in the next release. Is that correct?" You may be surprised how often a simple confirmation like this can uncover misunderstandings and avoid conflicts.

Setting up and confirming expectations in this way has another benefit: it sets up clear boundaries for contribution tasks. By defining what you will do, why, and by when, you create explicit limits for the deliverable. This helps to reduce scope creep on projects. Everyone knows what work needs to be completed for the contribution, and everyone knows what "done" looks like for that work. There's much less opportunity for adding new requirements to a task that has already been well defined through good communication and expectation setting.

As important as it is to set up and confirm expectations with the other members of the FOSS community, it's equally important to maintain those expectations. The world is a complicated place, often leading to expectations needing to change. Sometimes as you get going on a task, you learn that it's more complex than originally thought. Sometimes something happens in your personal or work life that requires you to set your free and open source contribution aside for a while.

The least helpful thing you can do when, for whatever reasons, you can't meet the established expectations of the community? Disappear and say nothing. Radio silence only amplifies the frustration and disappointment the community will feel when you don't meet their expectations. You may be quietly hammering away, trying to solve the problem, hoping that you can make some sort of progress that won't let them down, but what you're most likely doing is delaying the inevitable, making the community wonder what's going on, and depriving them of the chance to pitch in and work together to meet expectations. Staying silent about a need to change expectations wastes everyone's time and energy. Don't do it.

When you're working on a task and you learn that there's a question or problem that may lead to not meeting the established expectations, immediately stop and communicate that. Tell people when you have to push a due date by a week due to unexpected crunch time at work. Let them know that the feature you're removing will impact the project in unanticipated ways. Ask for help when you uncover something with which you're not familiar. The sooner you let the community know, the sooner the issue can be addressed and expectations can be reset, and the sooner everything will tick along smoothly.

Free and open source projects are built by people for people. They're all in this together and all there to help, but they can't if you don't let them know there's a problem. Do the right thing by setting up, confirming, and maintaining expectations in all your communications with the community.

Communication Channels and How to Use Them

OK, now that we have the general tips out of the way, let's start talking about some of the (mostly) unwritten rules of the various types of communication channels in use by free and open source projects. While every project does it differently (remember those Very Strong Opinions™ mentioned in *Prepare to Contribute?*), the majority of them use most of these channels in some form:

- Mailing list (*listserv*)
- Issue tracker
- Real-time chat
- Conference call

I'll provide you some general best practices for each method, so you won't have to start completely from zero, but always remember to check the project's documentation and CONTRIBUTING file to see which channel(s) that project uses and their preferred interaction styles on each one. If you can't find any information on how the project community prefers to communicate, send an email or open an issue asking this. Once you receive an answer, update the documentation accordingly. If you had that question, you can be sure the next new contributor will have it as well. By updating the documentation, you'll be helping the project and new contributors alike.

Mailing List

Most projects use a mailing list (*listserv*) of some variety. Very large projects use multiple mailing lists, depending upon their needs. They may have one for overall development of the project, another for user support, and then one just for announcements or community matters. However a project organizes its mailing list(s), you typically will find the information listed in the CONTRIBUTING or README file.

Mailing lists are a great channel for long-form discussion, particularly among the members of a distributed community. Not only does a mailing list encourage more thorough answers, but by slowing down the conversation, mailing lists help to level the playing field for all participants. The asynchronous nature of mailing lists gives participants the freedom to take their time to craft their interactions. People can read and respond to discussions on their own schedule, without the always-online pressure that sometimes comes with a channel like real-time chat (discussed later). Mailing lists are especially useful when a community is globally distributed or otherwise includes people whose primary spoken or written language is not the same as the primary language of the project. The typically slower pace of a mailing list puts these people—who need more time to translate their ideas—on a similar footing to those who fluently speak the primary language of the project and community.

A project mailing list also is a remarkable historical resource for all community members and users of the project. While the feature can be disabled, nearly all mailing lists are archived by default, and those archives usually are publicly available and searchable. If you ever wonder, "Why does the project do things this way?" you usually can find the answer in the mailing list archives.

As I mentioned earlier, some projects have multiple mailing lists. This might seem like overkill, but what it does is allow people to get only the information they need rather than the firehose of all emails related to a project. These lists usually share a common name but have suffixes to help tell them apart and denote what sort of content that mailing list contains. Some common suffixes are -dev for lists dedicated to discussion about the technical development of the project, -user for questions and discussions about and by end users of the project, and -announce as a low-traffic list containing important announcements about things like new releases, conference information, security warnings, and similar things, but no discussions at all. Check the project's documentation to see what mailing lists it offers and sign up only for those that are relevant to you. You can certainly sign up for all of them, but you may find you're receiving a lot more email than you want or can handle.

Writing a Good Email

Over the decades, a lot of (mostly unspoken) practices and etiquette have sprung up around FOSS mailing lists. With mailing lists being such an important part of the communication strategy for most free and open source software projects, being able to write an email that adheres to these practices is a skill that will help you communicate while also avoid annoying people by transgressing email etiquette. Here are some tips to follow when writing a new message to the listserv (*starting a thread*):

- Limit your message to a single topic and stick to it throughout the conversation.

- Use a good subject line. As they say in journalism: don't bury the lede. The subject should mention the topic you wish to discuss. Be brief and descriptive. If your question is about a specific issue, include the issue number in the subject line.

- Start the message with your question, proposal, or thesis and then (if necessary), spend the rest of the message supporting it.

- Keep your message text-only with minimal formatting.

- If you require additional resources for your message, save these resources elsewhere and then link to them rather than cut and paste the content into the body of the email. These resources can include images or screenshots, source code, error messages, stacktraces, among other lengthy or space-consuming things.

- While you can link to these resources inline where they're mentioned in the body of your message, it's usually preferred the links be referenced as footnotes in your message to help maintain the flow of the body of the text.

- Do not include attachments in your message. Many mailing list software packages have a maximum message size setting, and attachments will cause your message to violate that setting and therefore, not be delivered. Instead, link to the resource as described above.

Here's an example of a good mailing list message:

```
FROM: webdev@fossforge.com
TO: webframework-api-listserv@example.com
SUBJECT: page.lastupdate.datetime returns the wrong thing?

We're updating the theme for the website[0] and thought
it would be helpful for our visitors if each page showed
when it was last updated. I checked the documentation and
there doesn't seem to be an API method for getting this
information?

Then I dug into the source code for the page module[1]
and found that there's an undocumented method named
page.lastupdate.datetime.

When I called that method I got back a POSIX epoch
instead of a UTC timestamp like every other .datetime
method in the API. I dropped an example into pastebin.[2]

Should it be doing that? It's not documented, so it's
a little hard to tell.

--V

[0] https://fossforge.com
[1] https://gitlab.com/webframework/blob/master/source/
page/page.py
[2] https://pastebin.com/4cbeN8zj
```

Replying to a Mailing List Message

You would think that replying to a mailing list message is a relatively simple matter, but you'd be wrong. Many FOSS communities have strongly held opinions about what does and does not constitute a correctly formatted reply on a mailing list. It's very easy to transgress these rules, and it's very rare that they are ever written down. What follows are some of the most common rules for listserv replies, but as with everything with FOSS projects, you should do a little research before diving in. Have a look at the project's mailing list archives to see how most people typically reply and then use that as a rule of thumb for how to proceed with your own responses on mailing list threads.

First of all, there's the matter of *top post* versus *inline replies*. For various probably-not-nearly-as-important-as-they-seemed-at-the-time reasons, lots of FOSS participants have strong opinions about these two email formatting options.

You are likely most familiar with top-posting email replies. In a top post, you select a message, click Reply on your email client. The entire content of the selected message is copied into the new message buffer, you type your response above this without making any modifications to the rest of the buffer below your reply, and then you click Send. The user interfaces of several popular email services—such as Gmail and therefore, also Google Groups—encourage this type of message reply formatting. The email client handles hiding the copied content in the new message, typically behind some sort of *click here to see more*-type interface.

```
FROM: coredev@webframework.org
TO: webframework-api-listserv@example.com
SUBJECT: Re: page.lastupdate.datetime returns the wrong thing?

Huh. Yeah, that's a bit weird. Could you open an issue for that
(and one for the missing documentation)? We'll have a look.

Thanks for finding this for us!

Cheers,

Subha

On Tue, Jan 23, 2018, at 10:45 AM, VM Brasseur wrote:
> We're updating the theme for the website[0] and thought
> it would be helpful for our visitors if each page showed
> when it was last updated. I checked the documentation and
> there doesn't seem to be an API method for getting this
> information?
>
> Then I dug into the source code for the page module[1]
--click to see more--
```

Fans of top-posted replies appreciate that for any given message in a mailing list thread, they can always see the entire conversation that led to that message by clicking that *click here to see more*. There's no need to navigate to any other user interface to find the information they need.

On the other side of the email reply formatting coin you have inline replies. With an inline reply, you still select a message and click Reply to have the entire content of the selected message copied into the new message buffer. Instead of typing your response at the top leaving the rest of the message buffer intact, you edit the message buffer to type your responses *inline*, beneath the bit of the message to which your response applies. If there's buffer text that does not apply to your response, you remove it from your reply.

Fans of inline replies appreciate that placing the response directly beneath the statement provides clear and explicit context for each statement. They also appreciate that removing unnecessary text from the response creates an email message that's smaller and easier for them to skim. They often rely on the mailing list (or their own email) archive, should they require additional context or history for the thread.

```
FROM: coredev@webframework.org
TO: webframework-api-listserv@example.com
SUBJECT: Re: page.lastupdate.datetime returns the wrong thing?

On Tue, Jan 23, 2018, at 10:45 AM, VM Brasseur wrote:
> Then I dug into the source code for the page module[1]

That was clever of you. :-)

> When I called that method I got back a POSIX epoch
>
> Should it be doing that? It's not documented so it's
> a little hard to tell.

lolno. It totally shouldn't be doing that. Could you open
an issue for that (and one for the missing documentation)?
We'll have a look.

Thanks for finding this for us!

Cheers,

Subha
```

Many project communities culturally prefer one type of reply over the other, but few make that preference explicit in their documentation. Check the archives for the mailing list to see which of the two predominates in replies. If there doesn't appear to be a preference, use whichever of the two response formats feels most natural to you for the message you're trying to convey.

When replying to a message on a mailing list thread, keep the subject line as is. This allows people to skim their inbox for messages related to threads they're interested in. Yes, most email clients handle threading these days, but you can't assume how the reader has configured their client. There's an exception to this rule—when you want to start a new thread based upon an existing thread. In that case, change the subject line accordingly, but put the original subject in parentheses accompanied by was:. For example:

```
FROM: doclead@webframework.org
TO: webframework-api-listserv@example.com
SUBJECT: Time for a doc audit? (was: Re: page.lastupdate.
datetime returns the wrong thing?)

On Tue, Jan 23, 2018, at 10:45 AM, VM Brasseur wrote:
> Then I dug into the source code for the page module[1]
> and found that there's an undocumented method named
> page.lastupdate.datetime.

We've had a few of these reports in the past few months.
Is it maybe time to do an audit to make sure everything
is doc'd and that the docs are correct?

~Lew
```

Managing the Email Load

A common criticism of mailing list email is that there's just so darn much of it. A large project with several mailing lists can easily generate several dozen or more emails a day. This is a lot of noise, which generates a cognitive burden (a drain on your mental resources), decreasing your productivity and effectiveness. How can you subscribe to mailing lists without being overrun by all the noise? Simple: you reduce the noise that directly impacts you.

The first way you can reduce the noise is by subscribing to only those mailing lists that actually impact you. Modern technology has made it a lot easier for us to be plugged in to many different streams of information. This can lead to amazing insights, but it also leads to information overload. It can be tempting to subscribe to every mailing list that is even slightly interesting to you, lest you miss out on that one or two nuggets of wisdom that precipitate out every once-in-a-0000while. Before doing so, take stock of the impact the additional noise of that mailing list will have on your life. You have a limited amount of time in this world. Do you really want to invest some of it on the noise of a mailing list that doesn't really apply to you very much? Only you can make that decision.

If you must subscribe to mailing lists, the second way to reduce the cognitive burden is to get that listserv traffic out of your inbox. Every modern email service provides some sort of filtering mechanism, and if the one you use somehow does not, then you can often rely on a filtering feature in your email client. How you organize the filters, folders, tags, or whatever mechanism you use does not matter. The important part is to get those messages out of your inbox—which usually demands the highest level of your email attention—and into an organizing system that's easy to find, easy to skim, and most importantly easy to ignore when you have more important things to worry about. This compartmentalization helps immensely to reduce your cognitive burden and free up your brain for other things. Out of sight, out of mind.

The third way to reduce the cognitive burden of mailing lists is through selective participation (*skimming*). Do you really need to read every single mailing list message in detail? If you're just starting out in the project, you may want to. This can give you a good sense of the members of the community and how each interacts, as well as a sense of the challenges faced by the project and its community. However, once you're more familiar with the environment, you may wish to switch to skimming message subject lines rather than reading every message on every thread.

Either way, read or skim, you should spend more time on those activities than on replying to messages until you have enough experience and knowledge to make the good impression you'd like to make. Speaking when you don't understand just makes you look foolish. One exception is questions: If people are discussing a concept or topic you don't understand or for which you don't have enough context, ask for more information. Don't expect to be spoon-fed that information. Instead, ask for pointers to where you can find resources to help you learn more.

No matter what, try to participate only in discussions that apply to you. We sometimes put a lot of pressure on ourselves to participate in every single conversation, but there's rarely any need to do that. Again, remember that time is not a renewable resource. Where is your time better spent? It may seem blasphemous to say so, but just because someone may be wrong on the internet[5] does not necessarily mean you have to be the one to correct them. So skim those subject lines and only pay attention to the mailing list threads that apply to you. Don't worry: if your input is needed on another thread or list, someone will tell you.

Issue Tracker

While it's not typically considered a communication channel, a great deal of information is communicated through a well-maintained issue tracker. Each popular version control system—GitHub, GitLab, and BitBucket—offer their own issue tracker integrated into the rest of their service. Other issue trackers you may see include but are not limited to Jira, Bugzilla, Redmine, Trac, and OTRS. Some project communities prefer this communication channel to all

---

5.   https://www.xkcd.com/386/

others and will ask people to open issues for all questions and discussions. For them, the issue tracker provides a public record that's easy to search. Maintaining all discussions in the issue tracker means that a discussion can quickly and easily be converted into an action item, bug report, or feature request. By assigning issues to people, they're able to add accountability to discussions and tasks and help their community members track the discussions and tasks that they're participating on. Should an issue spark a heated or controversial discussion, many issue trackers have features, such as moderation or issue-locking, to help prevent the conversation from spiraling out of control.

This use of issue trackers, while gaining in popularity, is still the exception to the rule in free and open source software projects. The majority of projects reserve issues for action items, bug reports, and feature requests. No matter what, always read the CONTRIBUTING file and other documentation before using a project's issue tracker.

Opening a Good Bug Report

This is as good a time as any to broach the subject of issue quality: it usually stinks. We in technology seem to have a preternatural ability to write bad bug reports that is surpassed only by our irritation when faced with having to resolve and fix a bad bug report. That's OK; this is a fixable problem. I'm going to give you guidelines for opening a good issue, bug report, or otherwise. This is something you'll need to do for any project, so it's best that you start learning it now.

First of all, before you open a new issue for a free and open source project, search their issue tracker to see whether your issue has already been reported. It can be helpful to search both open (work not yet completed) and closed (work completed) issues, as it's possible that your issue either was fixed already but is not yet released or someone reported it, but the project maintainers decided it wasn't something that needed fixing. If you locate an open issue, add your information as a comment to it. If you locate a closed issue, consider whether you need to open yours at all. If you decide that, yes, this is still an issue that you'd like someone to work on or discuss, then open a new issue per the guidelines that follow and reference the closed issue in it. Do not re-open the closed issue or add a comment to it unless the project maintainers have directed you to do so. Comments on closed issues get lost or ignored, and re-opening closed tickets upsets project maintainers as well as their workflow.

Once you've determined that you need to open a new issue, give it a brief descriptive title. "API problem" is vague and not helpful to the maintainers who are reviewing and triaging the issue queue. "API method page.lastup-date.datetime returns epoch timestamp" is very descriptive. The title should briefly and uniquely summarize the detailed account that you'll include next. It shouldn't be too much longer than 50 or so characters (if you're using English). Longer than that and it becomes a burden to read. A maintainer should be able to skim through a list of issues and immediately understand an issue's general nature without having to drill down for more details.

The hard part is next: writing up the bug report description. These fields usually have no character or word limit (or have limits so large as to be effectively nonexistent), so feel free to take the space necessary to describe your issue completely. What does "completely" mean? That will vary by issue purpose. A support question may need one set of information, a feature request another. Generally speaking, the following information is always useful:

- What you did, what you expected, what you saw instead

- Steps to reproduce (if a bug)

- Platform, browser, or equivalent technical information

- Exact text of any error messages and codes received. Screenshots aren't searchable, so reproduce the error message in text form.

- If applicable, a screenshot of the bug to help provide additional context

Note: Each issue should cover only one problem or question. One issue, one question. If you see multiple problems or have multiple questions, open an issue for each of them. For instance, if you're having problems with a project's API, you'd open one issue for the API returning inconsistent data and a separate issue for the API method you're calling not being documented.

An example of a good issue:

```
TITLE: API method page.lastupdate.datetime returns
epoch timestamp

DESCRIPTION: The page.lastupdate.datetime method returns
a POSIX epoch timestamp. All other datetime methods in
the API (page.creation.datetime, user.creation.datetime,
etc.) return a UTC timestamp. This problem occurs when
the API is called on any page in the application.

EXPECTED TO SEE: page.lastupdate.datetime return a UTC
timestamp, consistent with other related API methods.

STEPS TO REPRODUCE: Call the page.lastupdate.datetime
method, passing it the name of page in the application.
```

At all points, be precise, polite, and respectful with your words, even if the software has crashed and lost you a week of work. Until the maintainers have had a chance to dig into your issue, you have no evidence that the software is to blame for the crash (it could have been the configuration of your computer), and really, you can't get angry at the software or the maintainers if you haven't learned to save your files more frequently. Always work to maintain a respectful demeanor when reporting and commenting upon issues. These people are volunteering their time, after all, and one day you may be the one on the receiving end of the issues for the project.

Many projects have their own specific guidelines for opening issues. Some issue tracker software allows project maintainers to define issue templates to ease and enforce those guidelines. If a project has taken the time to establish guidelines and/or issue templates, use them and follow all instructions per the community's preferences. Neglecting to do so will just annoy the project maintainers and make it much more likely your issue will be ignored rather than resolved.

Maintaining an Issue

Issue maintenance is an important but often neglected facet of the software development process. Each issue reflects a hypothesis, followed by a series of experiments that either meet the goal of the issue or do not. Therefore, when working with issues, think of yourself as a scientist and the issue as your lab book. Scientists track everything they learn throughout the course of their experiments, not only for their own future reference, but also so that other scientists can learn from and potentially contribute to their findings. What sorts of things does a scientist track?

- The hypothesis to test and the method they plan to use to test it
- How to perform the test, what the outcome was, and why it happened
- The current state of the hypothesis after the test and the expected next steps

Much like a scientist, you should track your hypotheses, tests, and results when you work on an issue. By doing this, you build a body of information from which others can learn. You also enable an easier handoff of an issue. The next person to work on it can see what was done, why, and how it worked out. This minimizes duplicate effort, making the best use of everyone's time. If you hit a problem you can't overcome, having good notes of what you've already tried makes it much easier for another community member to join you on the issue to help troubleshoot. They can review your previous work and point out any incorrect assumptions you may have made along the way.

And let's not forget the most frequently used feature of good issue notes: allowing you to remember what in the heck you were doing before you got distracted by something else. Be it a day, a week, a month, or even just an hour that you're away, having your train of thought and progress documented will save you a lot of frustration.

Tracking this information is as simple as adding a note in a comment field on the issue you're working on. It doesn't have to be anything formal. Just make note of what you're trying, why, and the results you see. For instance:

```
Testing on my local install. Just using curl because it's
quick and easy and I just want to see what the method
returns.

Pliny:webframework brasseur$ curl http://localhost/index/
lastupdate/datetime
{
    "name": "index",
    "type": "page",
    "properties": {
        "lastupdate": 1062313200
    },
}
```

```
Yup, that's definitely an epoch right there. OP is right
that this should be a UTC like all the other datetime
methods. I'll have a look at the code after lunch.
```

Is it a lot of work maintaining an issue in this way? Maybe. It can be difficult for some people to get used to adding this issue maintenance step to their existing workflow. Will you ever regret the effort required to fully document your work on an issue? Never once. Will you regret not doing it? *All the time.*

When Is an Issue "Done"?

The answer to the question, "Is this issue done?" may seem obvious. I mean, there's a problem, and then you fixed the problem, and then you submitted the contribution, and now the issue is done, right? You can close it and move on, yes?

No.

Unless you're already familiar with a project's issue life cycle, never close an issue unless someone has told you to. While your piece of the issue may be complete, there may yet be more work to do. The fix may need to go to someone to document, or it may need to be packaged up for distribution. It may need a security review. Perhaps the project keeps issues open until the fixes in them are shipped in a release. No matter what, there's always the reality that your fix will probably need to be reviewed. Each of these things (and possibly many other project management-related events) may require that issue to remain open and active.

So, you see, the question of "Is this issue done?" is actually a complicated one, and the answer will vary from project to project and from issue to issue. Therefore, never close an issue unless you know for sure that doing so is entirely in line with the project's workflow.

Real-Time Chat

Internet Relay Chat (IRC)[6] was invented in 1988 by Jarkko Oikarinen, and real-time online chat has been a cornerstone of free and open source software communities ever since. While IRC was probably the first chat system used by FOSS communities—and is still very popular—it's far from the only option available. Mattermost, Matrix, Rocketchat, gitter, Zulip, and Riot.im are a few of the many chat options used by free and open source projects.

Real-time chat enables...well, it enables chatting with people in real time (no big surprise there). Despite that, chat is actually both synchronous and asynchronous in nature. While you can use chat to have very involved real-time conversations with someone on the other side of the world, you also can leave messages to which others can reply later when they're available. This dual nature of real-time chat makes it a very powerful and flexible tool for coordinating a community of people distributed across time zones and schedules.

The synchronous-asynchronous duality of real-time chat means that it can be hard to tell whether or when someone will be available for a conversation. The "real-time" in "real-time chat" is somewhat deceiving, since in the case of free and open source community chat systems, it's usually safest to assume that all conversations will be asynchronous. You never know when someone has to step away from chat to take a call, a meeting, or their child to school. Often they'll be in a far flung time zone from you, so you may have a question while they're sleeping soundly in their bed. None of this means you can't still start the conversation and leave it there in the chatroom, ready for them to see when they return. Simply mention their chat username in your message, and it'll notify them so they won't miss it.

As I mentioned in *Prepare to Contribute*, the selection and use of a real-time chat system has taken on nearly religious significance in some free and open

---

6.   https://opensource.com/life/16/6/irc

source software communities of late. Respect the chat option that your community has selected and do not start a contentious discussion by suggesting they switch to another, unless you have a very good reason for doing so. Rest assured that no matter what chat system is in use by the projects in which you participate, a great deal of conversation (and possibly arguments) went into its selection and maintenance.

How to Use Real-Time Chat Effectively

You may think you're familiar with how to use a chat system, but there are a number of points of chat etiquette that FOSS project communities have developed over the years, and they may not match what you're used to with other chat systems.

If the chat system in use offers multiple chatrooms or channels for the project, pay attention to the topic of each chatroom and stick to that topic during all of your conversations in that room. Off-topic conversations can make it difficult for people to keep track of the important conversations going on in that chatroom, so if you must have an off-topic conversation, move it to a different room or channel.

Some chat systems such as IRC feature the ability to include URLs in the topic for a chatroom or channel. If a topic contains URLs, click through and read those pages. These typically point to documents relevant to the chatroom, including documents for discussion, rules for engaging on the chatroom, or the Code of Conduct for the project. Disregarding these URLs may lead you to violate chatroom policy and may get you kicked out.

The first time you enter a chatroom or channel for a FOSS project, take time to lurk silently before you participate in discussions. In a chatroom context, *lurking* means joining the chatroom and reading what's said there but not participating in the conversation yourself. This quiet observation will allow you to get a sense of the chatroom culture, its mores, and its interaction styles. Think of it as getting to know the language when you visit a foreign land. Even a little bit of effort to learn how the locals communicate enables you to navigate the environment more easily.

It's common for the first chatroom messages from people new to free and open source to be something like, "May I ask a question?" To most of us, this is simply being polite, the chatroom equivalent of raising your hand to speak in class. For experienced FOSS chatroom or channel members, your polite question is unnecessary noise. The purpose of chatrooms is to encourage questions and dialogue around them, so the permission to ask a question is assumed and therefore unnecessary. The phrase you may see used is, "Don't ask to ask; just ask." In other words, rather than politely asking for permission to ask your question, simply politely ask your question instead.

Because of the synchronous-asynchronous duality I mentioned earlier, chats will continue even when you're not around. Those accumulated chats are known as the *scrollback*. Depending upon the chatroom and the conversations, scrollback can sometimes reach several hundred lines or more in length. You're not obligated to read all of that scrollback if you don't wish. You may miss something, yes, but if there's something important for you specifically in there, then someone will have mentioned you in that message. This mention, also known as a *ping*, typically notifies you that you have a message waiting. Most real-time chat clients have a way for you to jump directly to your mention in the scrollback, so you don't necessarily have to go through all of it to find the relevant parts. However, you may find you need to read the scrollback anyway so you can get the context of the conversation.

When engaging in a discussion in a chatroom or channel, use complete sentences and spell out words rather than use abbreviations or "text speak." Also, try to use as good of grammar as you can, including correct capitalization and punctuation (it's OK; none of us are perfect on this front). Real-time chat is a textual communication channel, and the people sharing the chatroom or channel with you may not understand you well or respect your input if it doesn't appear that you even tried to construct it to be as readable and as understandable as possible. It's also likely that their primary written language is not the same as that used in the chatroom. Using poor grammar or abbreviations makes it difficult if not impossible for these valuable people to help answer your questions.

While we're on the subject of how to format your communications in a chatroom, PLEASE DO NOT USE ALL CAPS UNLESS YOU INTEND YOUR WORDS TO BE SEEN AS SHOUTING. We all need to yell from time to time, but try to keep it to a minimum. You don't want to become known as that mean shouty person.

Above all, when engaging in discussions on a FOSS real-time chat system, be patient. The community members of the project are most likely all volunteers, each with their own life and obligations outside of the project. A large percentage of them may even be in completely different time zones from you, such that your waking time is while they're fast asleep. Ask your question, then if you must, wait several hours for someone's schedule and life obligations to allow them to check the chatroom and reply to you. If after several hours, you still have not heard from anyone, ask your question again. If you still don't hear from someone in a few hours, it could be that the chatroom is not the best way to communicate with the members of that community. Check the CONTRIBUTING or README files for other communication channels for the project.

Conference Call

Once in a while, it makes sense for a project community to get people together for real-time, high-bandwidth communication. While meeting in person is great for this, it's also cost and schedule prohibitive. When you have community members distributed not only across the globe but also across the life-obligation and expendible-income strata, you can't really bring them all to a single location so you can have some quality brainstorming time.

While time zones are still a complication (which, if you work with software, is something you should get used to), a conference call allows the distributed community members of a project to come together and share their thoughts while also getting to know their fellow contributors in a way they never could through any other communication channel.

The tool used for these calls will vary by project and also by the bandwidth requirements of the members. It may not make sense to hold a video conference if many of the community members live in a bandwidth-constrained region or must pay a great deal for data plans for their mobile devices. Therefore, you'll usually find that conference calls for free and open source projects feature the option for voice-only participation so as to include as many of the community members as possible. Without this, it would be difficult to meet the goal of the call: to enable the community members to collaborate and discuss matters both remotely and in real time.

Conference Call Etiquette

As you can imagine, getting people together on a conference call is a fairly special event for most FOSS projects. There are a few things you can do to make sure the group is able to make the most of the limited voice-/face-time that they'll have together during the call.

Dial into the call itself several minutes before it's due to start. This allows you to confirm that you have the correct dial-in information with enough minutes to spare to frantically email or message people in case you don't. If the call is using an online service of some sort, connecting a few minutes early gives you the chance to download any necessary software or updates and have everything running smoothly before the call starts.

If you're the one organizing the call, always have an agenda for it. This lets people know what you plan to discuss so they can prepare in advance. It also lets people who aren't interested in those topics opt out and skip the call entirely. If you're not the one organizing the call, pay attention to the call agenda. Prepare information you might need in advance. Don't derail the call by changing the conversation to a different topic. Doing so is disrespectful of the time of everyone else on the call, who joined expecting to discuss what's on the agenda.

When you're on the call, always mute your microphone unless you're speaking. Even the tiniest background noises can disrupt a call, which wastes the time of everyone who's participating. If you've joined the call audio-only, without a video component, always state your name when you start speaking: "This is Vicky. I understand what Percy is suggesting, but I have concerns..." The community probably doesn't get the chance to get together very often, so don't assume that they can recognize your voice.

Only the Tip of the Iceberg

This chapter has covered a lot of the mostly unwritten rules about how to interact in free and open source software communities. By now you can probably guess that the applicability of these rules depends upon the project, the community, and its culture and preferences. Use this chapter as a guideline, but always follow the established communication norms for the project.

Now that you know how to communicate with others in a FOSS community, it's time to get to know them, and what better way to do that than getting together in person?

CHAPTER 8

It's About the People

By now you've noticed a large part of the book is dedicated to methods and tips for interacting with others. That's because the most important aspect of free and open source software isn't the code; it's the people. Contribution to FOSS is about so much more than simply code, design, or documentation; it's about participation and community. The licenses make the software available, but the people make the software, and the community supports the people. Remove one piece from this equation, and the entire system falls apart.

The interactions between contributors lead to innovations, true, but more importantly, they lead to lifelong collaborations and friendships, often with people who live on the opposite side of the world from you. While these relationships can be fulfilling and inspiring, they take work to get right. This chapter will help you learn how to get together with and relate to your FOSS community. Those get-togethers can be a casual meetup or a big international conference and everything in between, and each type will have its own guidelines. Most importantly though, this chapter will help you navigate the mostly uncharted waters of FOSS communication. A lot of shoals lie just below the surface, and if you don't know to look for them, you and your FOSS career may end up a complete wreck.

Get Together

One of the best parts of contributing to FOSS projects is getting the chance to meet up with your fellow community members. These gatherings sometimes draw people from all over the world. They give you the opportunity to meet people and learn from them. Face-to-face meetings help to build trust, create and strengthen friendships, and increase empathy with others. This last point is often overlooked but very important. According to an article by *Laura Delizonna [Del17]*, empathy among team members has been shown to improve communication and productivity by creating a space of psychological safety. It also has a welcome side effect of helping us become better human beings, which is something we all need.

Sometimes these meetups take the form of a conference or event. Not all large, free and open source projects will hold a conference, but if they do, the event tends to be quite large and international in scope. *DebConf*—for the Debian Linux distribution—and *ApacheCon*—for projects supported by the Apache Software Foundation—take place yearly and draw several hundred attendees each. The OpenStack community holds multiple events each year. The *OpenStack Project Teams Gathering* (PTG) also occurs twice a year. Focused purely on design and development of the next version of OpenStack, the PTG attracts many hundred community members and contributors. The *OpenStack Summit*—held twice a year—regularly hosts many thousand attendees and is one of the largest FOSS-related events in the world. The actual largest event of that kind is *FOSDEM*. Unlike the other events, FOSDEM does not focus on a single community or technology. Instead, it welcomes all people interested or participating in free and open source software. Each year, more than 6000 attendees from all over the globe migrate to Brussels, Belgium at the start of February to learn from and meet with their fellow FOSS enthusiasts.

A meetup doesn't have to be a large undertaking with hundreds or thousands of participants. Many towns and regions are home to local meetups or user groups dedicated to FOSS projects and technologies. These groups can be very helpful. Not only can they introduce you to new projects, the group members are usually glad to help should you get stuck while contributing. Where do you find these groups? Meetup.com[1] is a good place to start. Select the closest city or region and search for open source. You also can search for a specific project or technology, like Linux or Python. This may turn up a few options for you, but if it doesn't, don't worry. There are other ways to locate groups. Most public libraries have community spaces where groups not only meet but also can advertize. If your library doesn't have such a space, ask the librarian whether they know of any local technology groups. Librarians are an amazing and under-appreciated source of local information like this. If your area has universities, colleges, or other learning institutions, drop by sometime and check out the bulletin boards near the department offices, career development center, student union, and library. These learning institutions may also offer online postings for groups. Online or off, the learning institutions in your area will likely provide many options for groups you can check out.

---

1.   https://meetup.com

Sometimes you can find a mixture of the two: smaller, more specialized, or more localized events collocated at a much larger conference. *Linux.conf.au* (LCA) and *PyCon AU* each host smaller events (called "miniconfs" by LCA and "specialist tracks" by PyCon AU) in the days before the main conference. Linux Foundation's *Open Source Summit* conferences, which occur multiple times a year at different locations across the world, frequently encourage collocation by smaller events, such as single-day summits devoted to diversity, business, or networking. *Southern California Linux Expo* (SCALE) typically hosts smaller specialized events before the main conference begins. Most free and open source-related or other technical-type conferences will also encourage smaller groups to use the event facilities in the evenings. These smaller meetups often go by the name *Birds of a Feather* (BoF) or *Open Space* sessions. So if there's a conference happening near you, have a look at its schedule. Even if you don't wish to attend the conference itself, the satellite events orbiting around it may be worth checking out.

Benefits of Face-to-Face Meetups

Small or large, local or global, regularly or just once, however you do it, I encourage you to attend some sort of face-to-face meetup with your community if you can manage it. You can learn a lot from online interactions, but there's nothing quite like sitting next to someone and chatting while sharing a basket of chips.

While face-to-face meetups are definitely a great opportunity to meet new people and make new friends (and eat chips), they offer a lot of practical benefits as well. For starters, these meetups will be the best place to meet the core or experienced contributors for the project. Large meetups such as conferences are where you'll find the highest concentration of contributors, and therefore, the most opportunities to learn. Meeting these people face to face is a great opportunity to receive mentoring. Many events feature hands-on hacking sessions, where you can collaborate and learn from the experiences of those around you.

In *What Free and Open Source Can Do for You*, I talked about how FOSS can benefit your personal network. Face-to-face meetups are the ideal place to make that benefit a reality. Large event or small, you'll have the opportunity to meet people you'd never have had the chance to, otherwise. Large events in particular can expose you to community members from all over the world. The diversity of people you can add to your personal network is truly incredible and can lead to many inspiring conversations and brainstorms. It also can lead to finding your next job, or if you're hiring, your next team member.

Overall, any sort of gathering of the project community provides the opportunities for planning, working, learning, and bonding that purely online interactions can't equal.

Down Sides of Face-to-Face Meetups

However great they are, face-to-face meetups aren't all sunshine and puppy dogs. There are some down sides to them, especially to the large conference-type events.

The primary downside is that these events can be very expensive to attend, putting them far out of reach of the majority of the community. Expenses can include travel to get to the event, hotel during the event, food while you're there, and registration fees even to get in the door. These are just the obvious expenses; others like childcare may also come into play. Often a community can provide some sort of financial assistance to help a few people attend, but if that assistance exists, it's likely to be quite limited.

There is no assistance program for the less obvious and often more difficult expense required for attendance: time. Many people aren't able to step away from their jobs, school work, or families to attend a meetup of any sort, large or small. Some smaller meetups and conferences try to schedule events in the evening or on weekends in an attempt to include more people, but there will never be a way to satisfy the schedules of every community member who wants to attend.

Another downside of face-to-face meetups is that often, they're just so darn overwhelming. There's so much to see and do, so many people around, and for new community members, so much that's unfamiliar. Combine all of these factors and a face-to-face meetup can be very intimidating and uncomfortable for some people.

Tips for Coping at a Conference or Meetup

There's not much to be done about some of the downsides of a face-to-face meetup (such as the various expenses involved in attending), but tips for how to cope with and thrive at one are many.

Even if you're used to them, larger meetups like conferences can be quite overwhelming. Some people can dive right in with no problems at all, but others are less comfortable and need a bit more time to acclimate. There's absolutely nothing wrong with either approach, so use whichever works best for you. The goal of these community meetups is to learn, get work done, and get to know people. You can't do that if you're forcing yourself to approach the event in a way that doesn't work for you. Whatever your approach, the following are tips that can help you get the most out of your community conference.

Use the Buddy System

If you're relatively new to the project and the community, or if you've never attended this event before, rest assured that you're probably not the only one. Consider using the buddy system to make the community conference more enjoyable. Having a buddy (or buddies; there's no need to limit it to just one) makes the event less intimidating and easier to navigate. Even if you know no one else there, you and your buddy can share tips, advice, leads on conference events and can conspire to find all the best conference sessions. With the buddy system, you'll always have someone to eat with and walk with, which can make attending a new event much more accessible. Buddies can also keep an eye on each other and call attention to potentially unwise choices, like staying up too late the night before an early flight or drinking too much.

Finding a conference buddy is easy: just reach out to the community, let them know you're new, and ask whether anyone would like to be conference buddies with you. You're likely to find that others are eager to have a little extra support for their first community conference, too. Depending on the community, you may even have experienced community members offering to become buddies with people who have never attended their conference before. This type of community collaboration leads to a much better experience and a stronger, more tightly knit community, and the friends you make in this way are often with you for life.

Networking Trumps Sessions

Officially, the primary purpose of all FOSS project conferences is for the community to get together, learn, and get some work done. This typically takes the form of a schedule of *breakout sessions* for active or passive learning in the form of tutorials, workshops, lectures, or led discussions, often arranged so sessions on similar topics are grouped into *tracks*. When you first attend a community conference, there's a very strong temptation to attend a session in every single slot on the schedule. This can work, but I'm here to tell you a secret: You don't have to go to everything. It's perfectly OK to skip sessions, if what you're doing instead is more valuable. What could that more valuable thing be? It's what's known as *The Hallway Track*.

The hallway track is what we call all of the learning that happens outside of the officially scheduled sessions. These are the conversations you have in the hallway, at the sponsor booths, or at the coffee station. Many people who attend conferences get so much out of the hallway track that they think it's the most valuable part of the event. You can learn a lot from the main sessions, but the hallway track is where you meet people and fall into interesting conversations that aren't as possible while you're sitting through a session. These conversations teach you a lot about the community, the project, and the industry. This is where you make friends, meet mentors, and maybe even get introduced to your next employer. While the main sessions can teach you a lot about the technical aspects of the project, the hallway track teaches you a lot about the people aspects, and as such, should not be missed. The most effective conference experience will include a healthy mix of both breakout session attendance as well as the hallway track.

Another name for the hallway track is *networking*. We talked about networking back in *What Free and Open Source Can Do for You* when discussing the benefits to your career. As a reminder: while computer networking is simply a method for computers to communicate, human networking is simply people communicating with other people. There's nothing special or tricky about it, but there are some things that you can do to make it easier.

For starters, carry and hand out business or personal calling cards containing your contact information. Yes, I know, this sounds a bit old fashioned in our digital age, but trust me: business cards are still very handy. They're highly efficient for sharing information quickly, effectively, without typos, and even in loud and crowded situations. Unlike mobile phones, a business or calling card will work when you don't have a signal or network. While a basic card is great, if you go that extra mile to get a good or clever design, it can help people remember you and encourage them to hold onto your card. Calling cards are also more secure. As the person designing and ordering the card, you get to control what information appears on it. Don't want to share your primary email address? Don't include it on the card. Don't want to share your phone number? There's no requirement to list it. Name, website, social networking usernames, PGP key fingerprint… Whatever information it is, you control what you share and with whom when you design your own calling card.

Another tip to ease the networking process is to keep some "canned" questions in mind, so you're always prepared to start a conversation when you meet someone new. These should be situationally appropriate, of course. While you certainly can start a conversation at a FOSS event by walking up to someone and asking, "If you were a tree, what sort of tree would you be?", the conversation may not go as well as you'd like. Innocuous but effective conversation starters should be simple, open-ended questions that prompt the other party to tell you something about themselves and hopefully give you some information you can follow up on. For example, here's the start of a possible conversation:

> *You:* Hi! I'm Anwar and this is my first time at this conference. How many times have you attended before?

> *Them:* Hi, Anwar! My name is Zikri. This is my third time here, but I've been contributing for about five years now.

> *You:* Wow, five years? I'm still pretty new to the project. What parts of it do you work on?

Other simple canned questions you could try include:

- "How far did you travel to get to the event?"
- "Do you contribute to any other projects?"
- "What's been your favorite session so far?"

As you're standing around in the hallway track, meeting new people and starting new conversations, consider using the *Pac-Man Rule*.[2] Popularized by Eric Holscher, a founder of the ReadTheDocs open source documentation service and the WriteTheDocs technical writing conference, the Pac-Man Rule simply states that for any conversation circle, the participants leave a gap. This makes the circle look like the Pac-Man video game character, which encourages other people to drop into the conversation. The Pac-Man Rule is a very low-key but effective way to make people feel welcome and included at busy events like free and open source community conferences. If you see a conversation Pac-Man, feel free to step in and listen to what folks are saying, then contribute to the conversation yourself once you're up to speed.

As useful as it is to learn how to start a conversation at an event, it can be just as useful to be prepared with ways to end one. We may all want endless time and attention span, but none of us have it. While you may wish to stand around all day talking about the technical, social, or political details of the FOSS project, you still need to get stuff done. And let's face it, not every conversation is going to be interesting. That's OK! It's perfectly fine to extract yourself from a conversation (be it pleasant or not) to move on to the next session or conversation, as long as you do so politely. Abruptly turning around and walking away may seem efficient, but it usually sends an unfriendly message. There are plenty of polite ways you can exit a conversation. For example:

---

2.   http://ericholscher.com/blog/2017/aug/2/pacman-rule-conferences/

- (Check the time) "Oh, I want to go to a session soon. I'll catch up to you later, OK?"

- "Do you know where the toilet is?"

- "I have some work I need to look at today. Hopefully I'll see you around later?"

- (Check phone, whether you received a message or not) "Oh, I need to take this message. Thanks for the chat!"

Ideally you'll tell the truth as you withdraw from the conversation, but if a little white lie gets you out of talking about a boring or uncomfortable topic, then by all means do what you need to do to take care of yourself while not burning bridges with the others in the group.

But Self Care Trumps Everything

Which brings us to the topic of *self care*. It's tempting to spend every moment engaging with your fellow community members, but doing so would be a mistake. Sure, you can power through the event on minimal sleep, minimal food, minimal bathing, minimal breaks, and maximal alcohol, but I guarantee you won't have nearly as good of an experience. You've probably invested a lot of time, effort, and money getting to this event. Why throw that all away by unnecessarily overextending yourself? You won't make a good impression if you're looking, acting, and smelling like a zombie while you're speaking with others. You won't retain information if you're running on no more than a catnap and good intentions.

Therefore, be sure to take care of yourself while you're at the event so you can perform at your best. FOSS community conferences and events should be approached like an athlete running a marathon, not one running a sprint. Pace yourself and give yourself the energy you require to reach the finish line. There are many ways to do this, but the four most neglected elements of conference self care are food, water, sleep, and mental space. Each one is necessary to keep your brain running strong.

There are calories and then there are *calories*. Any sportsperson will tell you that there's a difference between how much you eat and what you eat. While the scone you grabbed at the coffee vendor on the way to the event and all the beer you drank the night before do provide you energy to keep going, it doesn't exactly make for a high quality meal. Your brain needs more than sugar, fat, and alcohol to operate efficiently. A great way to ensure you eat at least one decent meal a day is to take it with others. Food is a great way to meet and bond with people you meet at the event. Not only can you strengthen the relationships you're building, but you also get to strengthen your brain at the same time.

Water intake is the next element that most people neglect when participating in a FOSS conference environment. Drinking enough water can make up for a lot of other self-care oversights, such as not eating, not sleeping, and drinking too much alcohol or caffeine. I'm not going to get into the definition of what "enough water" is, as I'm a FOSS specialist and not a healthcare professional. If you carry a bottle of water with you and sip from and refill it a few times a day throughout the event, you'll probably be in good shape. You can either bring your own reusable water bottle (they're very handy to keep around), or if it's an event that has an area for sponsors to exhibit, it's possible you may be able to pick one up at the event. If nothing else, you can always pick up a bottle of water at a shop on the way to the event and reuse that bottle. Once you start hydrating properly, you'll find your event energy is a lot more steady and reliable, allowing you to get through the day more easily.

While food and water will go a long way toward getting you across the conference finish line, nothing gives you energy quite like a good recharge. Sometimes you just can't resist staying up all night having wonderful conversations with brilliant and hilarious people. I encourage you to embrace those opportunities, but also to balance them with the rest you need so you can meet those people in the first place. No one gets as much sleep at a FOSS conference or event as they do at home, but that doesn't mean you shouldn't at least try to get several hours of rest every night.

Just as it's OK to skip a session to participate in the hallway track, it's also OK to skip out on events to give yourself a bit of a mental break. Free and open source conferences and events can be very busy endeavors. You're going to meet a lot of people and learn a lot of information, all in a very short period. To make sure you retain that information and don't burn out, take some time for yourself once in a while. Return to your room for a nap; go for a walk; find a quiet corner and write down some thoughts. Taking the time to process what you're learning will ensure that you're getting the most out of your time at the event. Some people also find so much condensed interaction to be very exhausting. Whether you're one of those folks or not, it's OK to withdraw for a little while to recharge your mental batteries before returning to the event. You don't need my permission for this, but now that you have it, feel free to take some "you time."

Some people may read the paragraphs above and think they're obvious. If you're one of those people: Excellent! It's rare to find people so in touch with themselves that they know and respect their own limits. Whether the tips are obvious or not, you must accept the consequences of your actions. If you don't eat, drink, or sleep well during the event, you probably have only yourself to blame for how miserable you feel both during and after it. You do you, honey.

Codes of Conduct

And speaking of freedom of action conjoined with consequences, let's talk a little more about Codes of Conduct. If you read *Prepare to Contribute*, you already know what a Code of Conduct is. If you didn't read *Prepare to Contribute*, I encourage you to do so now.

Not every free and open source conference or event will have a Code of Conduct, but it's generally a good idea to act as though they do. Many presenters and attendees (including me) avoid events that lack a Code of Conduct. I encourage you to follow your heart on that decision, as there is no right or wrong way to approach it. You have to do what's right for you.

If the event is covered by a Code of Conduct, it's very important that you read it, understand it, obey it, and if necessary, use it to ensure the safety of yourself and others. If you're ever at an event and find yourself wondering whether something you're about to say or do might violate the Code of Conduct, I encourage you to assume the answer is "yes" and either not say/do that thing or find a less controversial way to do so.

Even if you're someone who is positive that you'd never violate the Code of Conduct, it's worth taking a moment to review it. We all need reminders from time to time, not only of what's acceptable behavior, but also of why a Code of Conduct is necessary in the first place. It's not there to silence opinions. It's there to ensure that the event provides an environment that's welcoming to all, and that's a very good thing.

Form Your Own Meetup

Sometimes you can't make it to community events or conferences, and there are no meetups in your area. How can you engage with the community? By creating one yourself. You can always form your own group dedicated to learning about, sharing, and contributing to free and open source software. It's a lot easier to do than you'd think and can be very rewarding.

Local meetups are an excellent way to learn more about the project and its community. The members of a local meetup will have a unique perspective that you may not find in the greater community for your FOSS project. For starters, the local meetup members may share a language and culture different from the primary one of the project. This can make it a lot easier to share knowledge and support as you all learn about the project together.

Starting a local meetup doesn't have to be some big production. Sure, you'll probably see local meetups that occur regularly, host presentations by out-of-town speakers, and have companies sponsoring food and drinks for the event, but your meetup doesn't have to be that involved, especially not at first. Start small, if only to gauge local interest in the meetup before you invest a lot of time in organizing a more complicated and regular event. Start with a one-off meetup, gathering people at a local pub, library, or cafe to chat and see how that goes. This is a good way not only to gauge interest, but also to find people to help you organize something that occurs more regularly. It's good to have multiple people doing this sort of thing, as it distributes the responsibility and burden so no one person becomes overloaded and burns out. If only a few people show up: congratulations! That's a few more people than were gathering before, so you've successfully created a meetup!

If you've been to a FOSS meetup or conference before, you may have a picture in your head that your new meetup should follow exactly the same format: presentations by community members. Presentations are a good way to learn more about the project from your peers, and they can be as formal or informal as the group wants or needs. If you're just starting out with the meetup though, it can be difficult to line up presenters or a space that's appropriate for presenting. It often can take some time to get these things arranged, but that doesn't have to limit your ability to have a meetup.

"Hack nights" can be an easy-to-arrange and low-key format for a meetup. The basic idea is that the meetup members gather in a single location and work on contributions for the project or otherwise play around with it. Organizing an event like this is as simple as putting out a call to the community, letting them know where and when to meet, and possibly creating a theme for the event. A specialized theme you might consider is "New Contributors," where people who want to learn how to contribute to the project can get together, get their questions answered, and be supported by other members of the community.

Bug squashing, documentation writing, and testing a new release are all fun and easy themes, but there's really no need to have a theme at all. Sometimes the best type of meetup is purely social, with everyone getting together to chat and get to know others in the community. Having a shared FOSS project and community is a great ice breaker for this type of event, making it a lot easier for people to relax and hang out. Presentations, hack nights, social, or otherwise, feel free to mix, match, and combine meetup types to serve the needs of your local community.

As a new contributor, the thought of showing up to a hack night may be intimidating. There will be all of these people there, who all know more than you, right? I mean, you'd just be in the way, wouldn't you? You'll just slow them down. Nothing could be further from the truth. Hack nights are usually very informal, low-key affairs. While it's possible that there's a plan for what people wish to accomplish during the event, that plan is much more of a guideline than a rule. Because of the casual nature of a get-together like this, as well as the ready availability of skilled help, they tend to attract more newcomers and fewer experienced contributors. The people who show up to hack nights are always ready to answer questions and help other community members, even if they're new to the project. Simply grab your laptop, drop into the event, and tell people you're new. You'll be pleasantly surprised at the warm reception you receive at most hack night events.

Moving up in the Community

If you recall from *Prepare to Contribute*, projects often have a rough hierarchy of experience and responsibilities, which is sometimes represented as an onion:

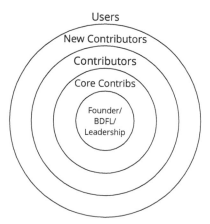

As a new contributor, you'll probably start out there near the outer edge of the onion, but there's no reason you have to stay there. Some people are motivated to progress actively through a hierarchy, while others are satisfied with a more casual approach. Both approaches are equally valid, so don't worry if you don't feel compelled to pursue a particular path. Whatever speed you prefer, if moving through the layers toward the center of that onion is important to you, there are some things you can do to help improve your chances (aside from the obvious step of "keep on contributing").

The best thing you can do to move up in the community hierarchy is to try not to do it all on your own. Communities are composed of people, and those people are there to help each other reach their goals. However, you can't necessarily expect people to notice that you need or want help. FOSS project development can be pretty hectic sometimes, and all of those people also have lives and jobs outside of the project. They're probably willing to help out but have not noticed that it's needed. The solution is for you to ask. This is pretty important: It's not their responsibility to lead you toward the center of that onion. It's your responsibility to take ownership for your own personal development. You don't inherently deserve to be in the center of the onion; you must earn it.

When asking for help, you can make a general request like, "Hey, does someone want to mentor me?" but you're more likely to get a better response if you're specific. Think about how you think you could improve your contributions; then ask for assistance with that well-defined problem. For example: "I would like to get better at doing code reviews. Could I pair with someone on one so I can learn what you look for when doing a review?" That's a well-defined request, and it has both beginning and ending conditions. Those busy people will really appreciate that, since they'll know they can help out without risking getting involved in an open-ended and potential time-sink of a situation.

As you're receiving help from others in the project, use that opportunity to ask them for feedback on how you're doing as a contributor and a community member, and ask them what they think it would take for you to reach the next level (whatever that may be for that project). Before you do that, you may want to go back to *Make a Contribution* and re-read the section about receiving feedback, since you may not necessarily be prepared to hear people listing your shortcomings. If you ask people for feedback in good faith, they will most likely provide it on the same terms. So do pay attention to what they have to say and try not to take it personally if you hear something you don't like very much.

During your path through the layers of the onion, make sure to speak with, ask assistance of, and in particular, be of assistance to the entire community. Don't simply aim your focus at those closer to the center of the onion and ignore everyone else. That sort of currying favor is not a community-minded action, and you'll probably offend most of the community by doing it. While the project cores are equipped to help and provide guidance, they're not the only ones. Everyone in the project community has experience to share and lessons to teach. You never know when a casual conversation with someone will turn up a recommendation for a handy new tool or a tip for a mind-blowing CSS hack. Keep your eyes open to help out with various tasks across the entire project and you'll gain a deeper familiarity with both the project and the community that supports it. This type of familiarity, more than anything else, is what will help you travel through the layers toward the center of the onion.

FOSS Is People

You'll hear it said frequently: Free and Open Source Software is People. No, this isn't some macabre reference to *Soylent Green*. While some communities are known for chewing people up (figuratively speaking), no humans are literally consumed in FOSS creation or maintenance. Without the people, though, FOSS is simply a bunch of lifeless code. The community is what gives that code life. People are the soul of free and open source software. Never forget that, and always try to think of the people when contributing. You're one of them now, after all. Welcome!

Sometimes, unfortunately, you'll find that your interactions with these people don't go as smoothly as you hoped. What do you do when it all goes wrong?

CHAPTER 9

When It Goes Wrong

Contributing to free and open source software projects is not all sunshine, puppy dogs, and roses. Plenty of things can (and will) go wrong along the path toward contribution. Some of these things are technical, such as build errors, difficulty in setting up the development environment, or having to learn a new technology. But it's more common for the roadblocks on that path to be human in nature, such as language barriers or hostile community members. In this chapter, we'll have a look at some of the most common things that can go wrong when trying to contribute to FOSS projects, as well as some ways you can overcome or avoid those problems.

Intimidated by FOSS' Reputation

The first roadblock you may face is that you may not feel up to contributing at all. Across its decades of life, FOSS has developed a bit of a reputation: It's difficult to contribute. You won't receive help even if you ask. The community members are unfriendly, judgmental, and unwelcoming. There's a pervasive attitude of "suck it up, buttercup, we did it the hard way and so should you." Community members are aggressive and insulting when faced with opposing opinions or imperfect contributions. The only way to thrive in FOSS is by having a thick skin and by "looking out for number one."

This is the reputation, and I'm sorry to report that it's based in reality. All of the bad characteristics I listed have occurred in free and open source software communities and undoubtedly will occur again. As you learned in *It's About the People*, FOSS is composed of people. As you've learned across your entire life, people can be difficult, complicated, squishy, and downright unpleasant at times. Therefore, any endeavor that involves people (so…you know…*all endeavors*) has the potential itself to become difficult, complicated, squishy, and downright unpleasant. FOSS is no exception.

It's true that many free and open source software communities have and do tolerate the sort of behavior that leads to all that unpleasantness, but it's unfair to paint all of FOSS with that ugly brush. Remember *that academic study [BBFV01]* I referenced back in *Make a Difference Without Making a Pull Request*? The one that shows that humans are more likely to focus on the negative than the positive? That same tendency is at play here. The overwhelming majority of FOSS project communities are helpful, supportive, welcoming, and grateful for their contributors, yet the few communities that tolerate negative behaviors become the bad apples that spoil the entire barrel and contribute more heavily to the overall reputation of free and open source software communities. Most communities, however, recognize that it's a bad idea to be jerks to other people and discourage and guard against the sort of behavior that's led to the poor reputation FOSS has gained over the years.

So, yes, there are FOSS communities that are nasty, brutish, and short-tempered. Overall though, you'll find that communities are composed of people just like you: normal folks just trying to improve the project and make a difference in their own small, yet significant ways. Don't be scared off by the poor reputation of free and open source software communities and be encouraged by the fact that your contribution is needed and valuable. If in your FOSS explorations, you discover a community that tolerates negative behaviors, the most effective thing you can do is to get out of there. You don't deserve to be treated that way, and they don't deserve your time, loyalty, or contribution if they think it's OK for their community members to be jerks.

Can't Find a Project

Another problem you may experience is not being able to find a project to which to contribute. You've read all of *Find a Project*, and you've done all of the exercises there, yet there don't seem to be any projects that meet your requirements and criteria.

If you think there are no FOSS projects that are a match for you, I confess that my first reaction is to raise a skeptical eyebrow à la Spock in Star Trek. Out of the millions of projects available today, there isn't a single one that meets your needs? While it's possible that this is the case, it's also unlikely. The odds are against you on this one, sorry. Yet the fact remains that you haven't located a project to which to contribute. So what's going on here?

Without sitting down and talking through the process with every one of you who have this problem—which you'll agree is an approach that isn't going to scale well—my suspicion is that your criteria and requirements are defined far too narrowly. Alternatively, you may be looking for a project that meets all of your criteria rather than just most (or even some) of them. Either of these constraints could lead to a very shallow pool of candidate projects, which is the opposite of what you want. While an entire ocean of candidate projects would be too much to handle, a shallow pool is not enough. What you'd ideally like to create is a decent little pond of candidates that you can wade into and splash around in a bit.

To get that nice little pond of candidates, you may need to open up your search criteria. For instance, if your criteria have you looking for projects only in one area of interest, try adding related interests to your list. If you like electronic music, maybe you'd enjoy working on a project for typesetting musical scores, or perhaps on a project for converting audio files between different file formats. Expanding your programming language options can help as well. Sure, you may not know Python very well, but if you're willing to learn, you'll find a whole new world of candidate projects opening before you, filling your little pond of options to the brim.

Once you have that pond of options, try to be less particular about which ones make your short list. Sure, it would be wonderful if you're able to find the *Perfectest Project Ever*, practically hand-crafted to suit your specific needs, but it's unlikely to happen. You'll probably find that most projects meet only a few of your criteria, and no projects meet all of them. That's OK! Even projects that only meet a few criteria still have the potential to help you move toward your goals. Just be sure you know which of your criteria are the most important to you, and which are just nice-to-haves. Try to focus your attention on the projects that meet the more important criteria, and you're more likely to be successful in finding a project that's a good fit for you.

Company Policies

As you learned in *The Foundations and Philosophies of Free and Open Source*, copyright is a complicated thing, but its concepts and those of intellectual property underlie every free and open source software project and contribution. You also learned that while sometimes you automatically have copyright over your creations, in some countries you must apply for it, and other times your employer retains copyright over anything you create while employed by them. This can be a big hurdle when you're trying to contribute to a FOSS project, because depending on your employment agreement, the work you submit to the project may not be yours to give. Submitting a contribution over which you hold no copyright is a recipe for legal disaster for you, for the project, and for your employer.

Who Owns the Copyright?

Before you start contributing to any free and open source project, it's imperative that you review your employment agreement first. If you can't locate your agreement, ask your HR department for a copy. Once you have it, confirm who owns your work when it's created in each of these situations:

- On company time and company equipment
- On company time but your own equipment
- On your own time but company equipment
- On your own time and your own equipment

Use this grid, marking in each box who owns your copyright for work created under each condition. Do you own it, or does your company?

Equipment

	Yours	Company's
Yours		
Company's		

(Time)

If it's unclear who owns the copyright in a certain condition, you have two options. First, you can take the safe route and assume that your employer always owns copyright to your work under that condition. You could try your luck by gambling and assuming that you retain copyright in that condition, but assuming in this direction could end up being very expensive for you. Your second option also costs money, but considerably less: take your employment agreement to a contract or employment lawyer and ask them to figure out who owns the copyright in each of the conditions in the grid. Ideally, you'll have done this before you start your employment. That's usually the best time to be negotiating any changes should you discover that each of the boxes in the grid come out saying, "Company owns", but it's sometimes possible to speak to your employer and receive permission to retain copyright over your FOSS contributions under one or more of the conditions in the grid. I'll talk more about that in a moment.

Once you fill in the grid and have a good understanding of who owns the copyright to your work and under what conditions, speak with your manager or supervisor and let them know you would like to contribute to a FOSS project. Even if you're contributing under a condition where you retain copyright, it's a good idea to let your manager know so they don't get surprised by this later. They also may not know who owns the copyright and under which condition, so it's best to get in front of that before it becomes an issue. It could be that your manager doesn't really care whether you contribute or not, but it's best not to assume (especially if you hope to contribute using company time or equipment).

Getting Buy-in

When you're speaking with your manager, ask them whether the company has an overall policy about contributing to free and open source projects. Sometimes, even if your employment agreement says otherwise, a company will allow its employees to retain copyright and contribute to certain projects. Other times a company may be OK with you contributing, but only if its done in the company's name or from the company's account. You'll never know until you ask, so do take a moment to gather this information.

If it turns out that, after all of this work, there's still no official way for you to retain copyright over your work and contribute it to a FOSS project, you may need to ask your manager whether it's possible to get an exception to your employment agreement and/or to the company contribution policy. Before you ask for this, prepare all of the business reasons that it's to your company's benefit to grant this exception. They're unlikely to do it out of the goodness of their hearts, because contributing is the right thing to do. You'll have to prove that the company will get something out of this arrangement and that your contributions will not put them at legal risk. If you're able to get them to grant this exception, get it in writing. Even an email confirming that you're allowed to contribute (and under what conditions) is enough to provide some protection should situations change later. For instance, you may move to a different team, and that manager may not know that you've been granted an exception to contribute. It's very helpful to have written proof of the exception so you don't get in trouble. However, don't rely on that exception not being rescinded in the future. Your past manager may have agreed to allow you to contribute, but your new manager may need you to spend your time in other ways.

CLA or DCO

This question of who owns the copyright to your potential contribution is particularly important when the project to which you wish to contribute has a Contributor License Agreement (CLA) or a Developer Certificate of Origin (DCO) that you must sign before your contribution will be accepted. If you recall from *Prepare to Contribute*, the CLA and DCO are legal documents used by some projects to help manage the copyright madness that can occur when multiple people hold copyrights in a single project. Each one of these documents requires that you agree that you have the legal right to provide your contribution to the project. It's very important that you be clear about whether you actually have copyright on your contribution before you sign one of these documents. Signing when your employer actually has the copyright can lead to a lot of very expensive headaches for you, the project, and your employer, and it may even lead to you losing your job.

It may not seem like that big of a deal who owns the copyright to the work you create, but as you read above, it can matter a great deal. It's not wise to play fast and loose with copyright law, and it's always a good idea to err on the side of caution. If you're not one-hundred percent sure that you have the copyright to something you wish to contribute—and if you don't have that in writing somewhere—do not take the risk and make that contribution.

Contribution Process Is Unclear

You've found a project, you've confirmed that it's OK with your employer for you contribute to the project, and now you're ready to dive in and get started! This is usually an exciting moment; you're all energized, motivated, and eager to start making a difference in the project. Unfortunately and all too often, all that energy fizzles away the instant you discover that the project doesn't have good documentation for new contributors.

The most immediate sign that a project's new contributor documentation is lacking is that it doesn't have a CONTRIBUTING file at all, or it has a file, but it's entirely empty (a common trend lately for projects hosted on GitHub in particular). That's a red flag that it may be difficult for you to make a contribution, but it doesn't necessarily mean that the project hasn't documented the new contributor process at all. Some projects put this information in their README file, so be sure to read that in its entirety before you get started.

Sometimes a project has a CONTRIBUTING file, but it's so sparsely populated that it doesn't provide much guidance to people who aren't already familiar with the project or with contributing to free and open source software. This is common in smaller projects and projects with contributors who've been doing this for a while. They've been contributing for so long that they've forgotten what it's like to be new to the entire experience, so they may no longer know what sort of information is needed to document the process for new contributors. For example:

```
# Contributing

If you want to contribute, just send a pull request.

## Coding standards

Lint your code and make sure it's PEP 8 compliant before
sending it to us.
```

This CONTRIBUTING file is meaningful (somewhat) if you have a lot of experience with programming or contributing, but isn't very useful otherwise. It expects that you know how to send a pull request, what *linting* is (let alone how and why to do it), what *PEP 8* means, and how to check that your code is compliant. It also doesn't provide any guidance about where to go if you need help or have any other questions, since it assumes you already know that the project uses its issue tracker for that sort of stuff.

What do you do in a situation like this, where the CONTRIBUTING file is light on details but heavy on assumptions and jargon? Start by researching all of the terms and processes with which you're not familiar. For this example, you might hit up your favorite search engine and learn about *linting* and *PEP 8*, or you may re-read *Make a Contribution* to refresh your memory on pull requests. There's also a glossary appendix at the end of this book that may come in handy. This research won't only teach you about unfamiliar concepts, it also will prepare you with the vocabulary necessary for further searches or to ask good questions of the other project members.

Asking questions is the next step in clarifying the contribution process. The research may give you enough information that you're able to start contributing, but it's likely there'll still be some gaps in your understanding (especially if there's no CONTRIBUTING file at all). You'll have to ask questions to fill in those gaps, but that can be a little tricky if the CONTRIBUTING file doesn't tell you where to go to ask those questions. Check the README file to see whether it mentions any mailing lists, real-time chat rooms, or other communication routes favored by the project community, then use that preferred route for your questions. If after checking CONTRIBUTING, README, and any other documentation, you still can't figure out how to ask questions of the project maintainers, open an issue in the project's issue tracker and ask your questions there.

No matter the communication route or the answers you receive, try to capture what you learn through your questions and your research in the CONTRIBUTING file. This helps reduce the questions that the next new contributor has when they start working on the project, not only making it easier for them to contribute but also saving time for the maintainers who now won't have to answer the same questions all the time.

If the project has no CONTRIBUTING file (or it's not useful) and if your questions about how to contribute go unanswered, consider finding another project to which to contribute. Your time and skills are valuable. Don't waste them on a project that makes it difficult for you to contribute. There are millions of free and open source software projects in the world. Share your time and skills with one that will appreciate and respect them.

Language Barriers

Sometimes the problem is less procedural and more lingual in nature. For example, what does the text below say?

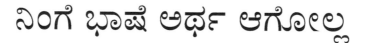

(Ninge Bhāṣe Artha Āgōlla)

Unless you read Kannada, a language spoken primarily in southwestern India and used by millions all over the world, it's unlikely that you knew that this text says, "You don't understand the language." If the image above just looked like a lot of lovely squiggly lines to you, then you have a sense of what it's like for the billions of people who could contribute to free and open source software but hit the human language barrier.

While FOSS is a worldwide phenomenon, the majority of projects use English as their primary spoken and written human language. It's the language most used for the documentation, code comments, mailing lists, real-time chat, and other textual communication for projects, but it's not the only language. If you search, you'll probably uncover projects that use your native language as their primary communication language, but right now your options will be limited if you look outside of English language-based projects.

No matter the human language of the project, if it's not one you understand, then you'll be at a disadvantage when trying to contribute. Your options for dealing with this issue are fairly limited: either you find a project based in a language you understand better, or you learn the language that your project of choice uses. I won't give you advice for how to learn a new language, since that's outside the scope of the book, but I will give you some advice on how to interact with and contribute to a project that doesn't use a language you understand very well.

For starters, it helps to set expectations by letting the community know that you're still learning the language. Usually people can tell if someone is not a native speaker, but it never hurts to be explicit about this. It doesn't have to be a separate message to the community (and is probably better if it's not), and it doesn't have to be anything complicated. As you first start communicating with the community, whether by the issue tracker, mailing list, or whatever makes the most sense for what you're trying to accomplish, just include a short line mentioning that you're learning the language. For instance:

> I have a question about running the test suite. Apologies for any errors in my wording. I'm still learning English. Please be patient with me. My question is...

As you're working to become more comfortable with the language used by the project, try to use asynchronous communication methods as much as possible. Email, issue trackers, and sometimes even real-time chat systems can all provide you with the time to think about and compose your questions and responses in a way that face-to-face conversations will not. This can help you gain fluency and practice in the language without adding the extra pressure of remembering the right word or form immediately.

It can be very helpful not to assume that you understand a question or statement. Before taking action on something, restate the question or statement and ask for confirmation. "I understood that we need to reorganize the documentation files into a single directory. Is that correct?" Taking a few minutes to confirm your understanding and the actions required can save everyone hours of work and many headaches later. If it turns out that you misunderstood what's needed, don't feel bad. It could be that the original statement or question was not clearly stated.

Relatedly, don't assume that your writing is as clear as you think it is. Languages and communication are complex things, and we all get them wrong from time to time. If you have a longer or a more important message you wish to send to the community, have a friend or another community member review it and make sure it actually says what you think it says before you send it off to everyone. Not only can this help your message be more effective, but it also gives you a safe space to practice and learn the language as you incorporate feedback from the reviewers.

It's worth noting that many of the tips apply even if you're fluent in the primary language used by the free and open source software project you've chosen. None of us are perfect and all of us need editors. Don't be afraid to double-check your understanding or your phrasings, even if you know the language. Doing so can help avoid a lot of confusion and streamline the software development process.

Your Contribution Is Declined

You've spent a long time thinking about and crafting your contribution. You're proud of your work here, or at the very least, you're eager to get it accepted so you can go on with your life. So you gather all the bits for your contribution, submit them to the project, and then...it gets declined. What gives? Why are they turning their back on your fine, hand-crafted contribution?

Before you get angry: Don't worry. Everything will be OK. It's not you, it's them. Or maybe it's you, but it's still OK (usually). There are plenty of reasons that your contribution may have been declined, and very few of them have anything to do with you personally or the quality of your work.

As I said in *Interact with the Community*, there are many reasons that a project may decline your contribution. Usually, the reason for declining it won't be a mystery. The project maintainers will probably leave a comment on the contribution or email you to let you know why they're unable to accept your contribution at that time. Some of the most common reasons for declining a contribution are:

- *The contribution appeared out of nowhere.* With very little to no advance communication with the project, they were caught by surprise by a contribution they didn't expect.

- *The contribution was good, but it wasn't necessary.* Perhaps you contributed something that's not on the project roadmap, something that the project maintainers had already decided they didn't wish to include, or something that someone else in the project had already contributed or was already working on.

- *The contribution was not to project standards.* Does the project have coding, testing, design, or writing standards? Did you check them before submitting your contribution? For a contribution that diverges greatly from the documented standards, it's often easier for project maintainers to decline it than to explain to the creator the many ways in which the contribution falls short.

- *The contributor has not signed the Contributor License Agreement* (or a commit for the Developer Certificate of Origin). Projects that require a signed CLA or DCO will not be able to accept contributions from unsigned contributors, no matter how good or useful those contributions may be.

- *The project members are mean.* It's very rare, but once in a great while you may come across project maintainers that won't accept your contribution simply because they don't want to. They have no good reason to decline it beyond not wanting to collaborate with others.

There are ways to prevent your contribution being declined or at least to prevent the decline being a surprise. If you've read this far in the book, you already know what they are: The three rules of free and open source software contribution.

1. Read all contributor documentation (and actually follow them).

2. Communicate and confirm before contributing.

3. Ask for feedback before submitting your contribution.

When in doubt, in any FOSS contribution situation, return to these three rules, and you'll be able to handle nearly anything...including having your contribution declined by a project.

Even after following these rules, your contribution may be declined, but you disagree with the reasons. Pause before replying. It's possible that you're feeling a bit emotional at that moment, and it's typically better in FOSS to act rather than react. Give yourself some time to calm down, then respond to the matter using facts rather than feelings. You may feel that your contribution is worthy of inclusion in the project, but if you can't prove that with facts then you're unlikely to change any minds and your contribution will remain declined. Remember though, that even if you do have what you feel are relevant facts, your contribution still may be declined and that's OK. Don't continue arguing simply because you have to be right, must win the discussion. Accept the judgment with grace, thank the maintainers for their time, and move on.

Community Problems

People, as I've already pointed out, are very complex, difficult, squishy things. Because communities are composed of people, they are similarly complex, difficult, and squishy. These factors contribute to communities exhibiting a lot of problems that, really, are common across most human endeavors. There are no perfect communities; there are only communities that recognize there are problems and work to fix them and communities that trundle along blissfully ignorant of their issues.

No matter which of these two types of communities you join, you're guaranteed to come up against problems that are based in human interactions and community culture. Often it's possible to work around these issues; once in a while it's possible to apply commitment and empathy to help fix them, and sometimes you may decide either just to deal with the problems or to leave the community and its problems in your rearview mirror. Which approach you take is entirely up to you, but it's important to emphasize that you do have a choice. At no point should you feel obligated to deal with or fix a community's problems. If you find that the community situation is uncomfortable to you, feel free to leave the community for a different one.

Unresponsive Community

One of the problems you may experience is that the community is completely unresponsive. You'll spend several very valuable hours creating a contribution, submit it to the project, and then...nothing. The community members never get around to reviewing your contribution, let alone acknowledging or accepting it. It's as though you tossed your contribution into a black hole, never to be heard from again. Other times they may respond, but it will take them weeks or months to do so.

There are plenty of reasons why a community may not be quick to engage with you, and none of them have anything to do with you personally or with the quality of your contribution. For one thing, there may not be very many people in the community. The fewer people there are to maintain the project, the more time it may take for any one of those people to review contributions as well as to submit their own. Each of those community members, no matter how many of them there are, is also busy trying to maintain their own life and the many complexities that come with that. Adding FOSS project maintenance on top of that is a burden that leads many community members to burn out and pay less attention to the project. This itself can lead to a project falling out of active maintenance. Any of these factors may contribute to a slow (or non-existent) response time when you submit a contribution or even simply a question to a project.

So what can you do about it? Before you submit your contribution, you can try to get a community member to acknowledge it and give you an estimation for when you might expect a review of some sort. This acknowledgment is usually easiest to get by email, real-time chat, or the issue tracker at the time when you're confirming that you understand the issue or that the project needs your contribution. Doing this up front before you even submit your contribution can help set up expectations on both the submitting and receiving sides of the relationship and can help smooth the entire process.

After submitting your contribution, you can gently prod people to remind them that a contribution is sitting there awaiting review. How long you wait to do this prodding will depend upon your needs, the project community's usual turnaround time, and other factors that vary from situation to situation. Typically it's polite to wait at least a week before giving the maintainers a nudge to see whether they've seen your contribution. However long you wait, do be polite when asking people to take time out of their day to review. You're unlikely to get the response you want if you're a jerk to the people whom you want to accept your contribution.

If weeks pass without hearing from the community, and if no other activity is happening on the project, it's possible that the project has fallen dormant for one reason or another. There are two options you can take here, but both of them may require a lot of work on your part. The first option is to try to contact the community and ask whether you can take over as lead maintainer of the project. This can breathe new life into a project, particularly when the existing maintainers are too busy or burned out. However, it's important to recognize that the project you're asking to take over is the one that contributed to that burnout. Think carefully before you take on that burden to make sure that you can bear it.

The second option is to *fork* the project, then use your fork instead of the original project: you create a separate copy of the project (a *fork*) and make whatever changes you need without having to wait for anyone to approve your contributions[1]. When you fork a project, there's no requirement to contribute your changes back to the original project as shown in the figure on page 140.

---

1.   https://opensource.com/article/17/12/fork-clone-difference

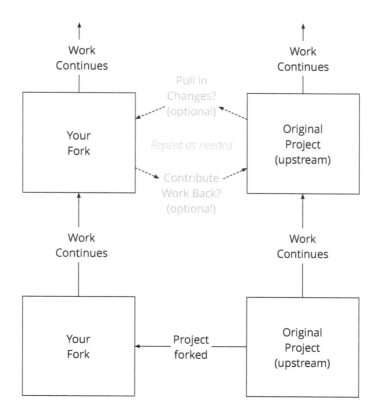

You might be thinking, "Great! I'll just do that and then I don't have to deal with those slow losers who won't acknowledge my contribution!" And, sure, that's one way to look at it. However, forking a project should be a last resort. It is almost always better to work *upstream* (on the original project) than it is to fork it to create your own version. If the project is still under active development, then it can be a great deal of work to keep your project in sync with upstream. Without this work, you're likely to miss vital bug and security fixes, as well as features that will make the project more useful.

Note as well that while some code forges like GitHub use the work "fork" as equivalent to a simple git clone of a repository[2], in this case, forking is a social move and can be seen as a hostile move by the original project's community. It can come across as you saying, "You're not doing a good enough job. I'm going to create my own project based on yours and build a better project and community, so there, take that." If you absolutely must fork a project, be careful how you approach it so you don't unintentionally cause offense. It's

---

far preferable to try to work with the community on the *upstream* project than create your own copy for your own personal use.

Overly Responsive Community

Once in a while rather than silent communities, you'll experience the other side of the communication coin: people just won't shut up about your contribution. Too many people communicating at once can be just as frustrating as no communication at all. In the case of an overly responsive community, you'll end up with far too many cooks in the kitchen. Each contribution received will have a host of people chiming in with feedback, each asking for their own preferred changes, and potentially each with differing opinions. This over-abundance of communication can make it impossible to get project maintainer approval for your contribution as you try to reconcile conflicting viewpoints.

While not always the case, an overly responsive community can sometimes be a sign that the project community is experiencing political problems or has little guidance or direction. Rather than collaborating to move the project in a single, agreed-upon trajectory, the contribution reviewers are each attempting to futher their own agenda or build support from other community members. Your contribution, unfortunately, is caught in the middle.

What do you do about the case of an overly responsive community? First ask yourself whether it appears they're aware of the problem. It may just be that there are no politics at play, and everyone is just trying very hard to be helpful in their own special way. Politics or not, the community may not realize that they're giving you conflicting information, overloading you with perspectives, or otherwise making it difficult for you to complete work on the contribution so it's ready for acceptance by the project. If this is the case, politely point out that you're getting conflicting information and ask them which way they would like you to go with it. When doing this, it can be helpful to summarize all of the perspectives. Often listing these in a single spot can show the reviewers how silly things may have gotten. For example:

> Hello! I appreciate all of your help and feedback, but I'm having a hard time reconciling some of the changes folks are asking for. Could someone please prioritize these requests or otherwise help me make sense of them?
>
> - Make the buttons blue to match the logo
> - Make the buttons the green accent color
> - Remove the buttons in favor of links
> - Merge this login page with registration and use those buttons
>
> Thanks for any help you can give me!

After studying the community, you may decide that this sort of consensus building isn't going to do the trick because matters are too chaotic or politically charged. There are a few other options you could try in this case. You could judge for yourself which is the most popular or prevailing opinion and focus on satisfying just it. Beware that this may have the effect of taking sides should there be a political struggle brewing, so make sure you're comfortable supporting the associated (or any) political agenda before deciding to go this route. Another option is to speak with a core contributor, pointing out the conflicting viewpoints you're receiving, and ask them to arbitrate the matter. Depending upon the project, the contribution, the conflict, and the overall situation, you may even wish to ask a core contributor to collaborate with you directly. This can help shield you from some of the politics and chaos and potentially speed up the process of accepting your contribution.

Unfocused Community

Do you know someone (or maybe you are someone) who can't seem to finish anything? They're constantly starting something new—new projects, new hobbies, new thoughts—but never actually seeing them through to the end. Some projects are like this as well. Lacking strong leadership or even a basic project roadmap, the community finds itself constantly shifting gears from one feature or initiative to another. There may be priorities, but they change frequently, and that change takes with it the time and energy that had been devoted to the previous "top" priority. People may be contributing a lot of work, but none of it is leading anywhere. For instance, the community may spend two months focusing its efforts on translating the user interface, only to set that work aside uncompleted as it changes course to focus instead on adding single-sign-on functionality. If your contribution is a part of that translation initiative, then when those gears shift, you may find yourself with a dormant contribution on your hands. It may be accepted, but it may never be used if the initiative isn't completed. This can be a problem if you need that initiative or your contribution released so you can use it at work or in one of your own projects.

When a community and a project lack focus, one way to handle it is to try to add a little on your own. It may be possible to gather collaborators from the community to complete the necessary initiative, or even to do so on your own if you have the skills and experience needed. By focusing your own efforts on a single piece of the project like this, you may be able to lead by example. As others notice, it might become possible to evolve the project toward one that's more focused and more likely to complete initiatives rather than abandon them for the *next big thing*. This will probably involve developing a project roadmap and/or a release cycle, and it will require project management and negotiation skills. Most importantly, it will require a large commitment in time and patience from you. This sort of change effort cannot be rushed if it's to be successful.

If you don't have the time (or patience) to lead or participate in the effort to evolve the project toward one that's more focused, your only other options are to become comfortable with the chaos and learn to work within the project's shifting tides of priorities, fork the project as described above, or leave that project in favor of another where your time and contribution will make a more immediate and positive impact.

Community Politics

As you probably gathered from the *Overly Responsive Community* section, free and open source software project communities can sometimes be politically charged. Frankly, any undertaking involving two or more humans can be politically charged, but FOSS maintainers, contributors, and users can be a particularly passionate bunch. That passion often leads to conflict, and the conflict can lead to politics or other complications. It's very true that not all politics is bad. Humans are, after all, political creatures, and we've done a lot of amazing things because of it. However, you all are probably also familiar with some of the less pleasant things that politics can cause in the world. FOSS project communities are no different and sometimes can suffer from the ugly type of politics.

The most common form of negative politics will be in-fighting between factions in a single project. This faction has one opinion, that faction has another, the faction over there...well, it's not clear what their opinion is, but they're against what the other two factions are trying to do. Another common form of FOSS politics is empire building by ambitious community members. For some people, being seen and acknowledged as important is a priority in their lives, as is amassing power. Even the small amount of power found in a FOSS project—such as setting a roadmap or approving changes—can lead some people to manipulate others and use both contributors and contributions as pawns to further their agenda.

When you join a project and discover that it chronically suffers from negative politics, you can of course try to stay out of it. You can send in your contributions, review submissions, and answer questions without picking a side. This can be very difficult, but it's possible. It's usually easier to evaluate the situation and then align yourself with a certain faction, but depending upon the situation, that may not be a desirable option either. If you find you can't participate in a project without also being a part of its community politics, but you don't wish to get involved in those politics, then your best option may be to withdraw from the community and go find one with less (or perhaps a different type of) political turmoil.

Rude Community Members

As I mentioned at the start of the chapter, free and open source software does not always have the rosiest of reputations. While part of that negative reputation comes from how difficult it is to contribute to some projects, the overwhelming majority of it comes from the fact that over the years FOSS has, does, and will play host to a lot of people popularly known as *assholes*. Some of you may object to the use of this word and its derivatives, and to you I apologize, but I will not change my vocabulary here. These people and their attitudes cause immeasurable damage, and I will not diminish that by softening my language. In this book, I will not hesitate to call an asshole an asshole. To do otherwise would trivialize how harmful they are to communities.

You'll find folks like this wherever people gather, but the less structured nature of free and open source software is fertile ground for these unsavory people. Without a central authority, common and documented guidelines for behavior, or a shared framework for dealing with unwelcoming behavior, these assholes feel justified in throwing the Golden Rule away and practicing their assholery with wild abandon.

This assholery takes many forms, but all of them act to make community members—and especially new contributors—feel unwelcome and uncomfortable, even when the actions are not directed at any particular individual. Some of the many different forms of assholery you may witness include:

- Ad hominem feedback that speaks to the person ("you're stupid") rather than to the contribution ("this isn't a good idea")

- Unnecessary negativity in reviews, feedback, and discussions

- Tearing down other people for no reason beyond entertainment value

- "Punching down," also known as attacking people that are lower in the community hierarchy

If this sort of behavior makes people feel uncomfortable and unwelcome, why don't communities do something about it? After all, a community is what it tolerates, so if that community tolerates assholes... Many communities have existed in this uncomfortable, unwelcome state for so long that it's become normal for them. They're no longer aware that this state is a problem, because it's simply "the way we do things around here." Some members of the community may be aware that there's a problem, but are unable to get the rest of the community to agree that it's something that they need to address. If they are able to gain consensus that something is terribly broken in their community, they then hit the roadblock of being unable to reach a similar consensus as to what to do to fix things.

Throughout this awareness-finding and consensus-seeking, the assholes are there too. While not always the case, often these people have risen to positions of power within the community. This position of power frequently has the effect of amplifying their unpleasantness as their position increases their confidence that they can do and say whatever they wish without repercussions. "They can't get rid of me," they think, "I'm far too important." Whether in a position of power or not, assholes are usually the loudest voices in the conversations about what to do about them. They are often clever individuals and are able to use rhetorical tricks to prevent the community from reaching consensus or taking action. These people turn the already difficult problem of community culture change into a nearly insurmountable task.

So what do you do when you come across a community like this, where certain bad apples truly do spoil the lot? If no one is correcting this behavior, or if the community does not have or enforce a Code of Conduct, the easiest thing you can do is to get out; withdraw from the community and go find one where assholes and assholery are not tolerated. As a new contributor, you're unlikely to have the power and influence to change a community that tolerates behavior like this.

The good news is that while there may be a bad apple in nearly every community, more and more communities are both implementing and enforcing Codes of Conduct. They don't tolerate assholes in their community, and they're doing something about it. There are plenty of projects of this sort where you'll be welcomed and your expertise and time will be respected.

How to Tell (Before You Join) That There May Be Community Problems

All that talk of assholes and assholery may be discouraging, but like I said, there are loads of projects that don't put up with that crap and where you can participate without fear of being treated poorly. How do you find them, though? How can you tell, without participating in the project, whether it's a good one or not?

Step one is to see whether the project has a Code of Conduct. If you remember from *Prepare to Contribute*, a Code of Conduct (CoC) documents the types of behavior that are both welcome and unwelcome in that project community, the consequences for unwelcome behavior, and where and how community members can report it. While a project having a CoC is not a guarantee that it'll be a welcoming and safe space for contributing to FOSS, it's a very encouraging sign. Alternatively, communities that don't have a CoC, or where the conversation about implementing one is very contentious, may be harboring and tolerating assholes. If a project doesn't have a Code of Conduct, be on your guard when joining the community.

Step two is to do your research and see for yourself how community members treat people. Review conversations on issues, skim the mailing list, lurk on their real-time chat system. These will give you an excellent view into how the project maintainers communicate and whether they tolerate unwelcoming behavior. You can see whether people are mean, impatient, or snarky when they respond to questions from others, or whether they're prone to ad hominem attacks or comments. You also can see whether community members respond to questions at all. While not responding may not be a sign that the community is unwelcoming, it's certainly not a sign that you're likely to get much help with your new contribution, either.

Step three is to ask around. If you know other people who participate in free and open source software, check with them to see whether they know anything about that community. You can learn a great deal about a community just by asking others what they've heard about it, even if only through the grapevine. Problematic communities get reputations, and often there's a whisper network that warns people away from the bad ones.

As you do this research, you may find that you're not very comfortable with what you learn about the community you'd planned to join. If that's the case, carefully consider whether you should still follow through on that plan or look for a more welcoming and less frustrating project to which to contribute. You pay for your FOSS contributions with your time, and that's the most valuable thing you have. Once you spend it, you never get more, so invest some of that time in discovering whether a community will treat you with respect. It's perfectly OK to change plans and take your skills and time to another project, one that will appreciate and respect you. You have the power to choose. Use it.

Sometimes You're the Problem

Sometimes, I'm sad to report, the asshole in the community is you. Some people have made a hobby out of being rude and disrespectful. I would like to think that you're not one of those people, but we all have bad days when we're rude to others (intentionally or otherwise). If we don't take steps to curb this sort of behavior, then we become that person about whom everyone else whispers behind their back, the one everyone dreads to have review their contribution, and the one that only other assholes want to sit with at community meetups. Do you really want to be that person? For most of us, the answer is, "goodness, no," but to avoid it, we all must be aware of our actions and their potential effects on others.

As a new contributor to a FOSS project, several actions can make someone look like a real jerk, on the fast track toward full-blown assholery:

- *They don't follow instructions.* There's a perfectly good CONTRIBUTING file sitting right there in the repository, but they choose to ignore it and go their own way with their contribution.

- *They send a contribution without confirming it's needed or wanted.* Because naturally no project community would be foolish enough to turn down the chance to have a contribution from them, right?

- *They work alone and isolated rather than collaborate with others.* Other people are such a drag, aren't they? Always making suggestions and questioning your judgment. They're just the worst.

- *They act on assumptions rather than facts.* No one's going to mind if they completely rip out and rewrite the entire object model of the code, honest. There's no need to double-check making a change like that, nope. They go ahead and assume everyone will be OK with it.

- *They talk down to people.* Look, folks, they've read every possible book on this subject and they know best. Would you just listen to them? Why are people so stupid?

In summary, any action in which a person comes across as arrogant, self-absorbed, self-serving, or abrasive is an action that makes them look like a Grade A Asshole. Every one of these actions comes from a lack of perception, awareness, mindfulness, and perhaps even caring how actions affect others. Once in a while, we all slip and do something insensitive like this, and that's not a problem as long as we're aware of it and take steps to make sure it never happens again. The problem comes when we don't bother to inspect our own behavior at all, let alone to learn from it.

This isn't a self-help book, and teaching you how to become a better person is outside of the scope here, so I won't go into that in any detail. I will, however, encourage you at all points to *Start With Yourself First*. If you experience a problem—personal, social, technical, or otherwise—when contributing to a

FOSS project or community, before looking around for someone to blame or somewhere to finger-point, turn that finger on yourself first. What in your behavior or actions may have contributed to the problem? What could you have done differently? How did your reaction to the problem improve or worsen the situation? What should you be aware of so this won't happen again in the future? How can you change your own behavior to create a more positive outcome the next time?

Ask yourself these questions regardless of whether your actions caused the problem or not. Get into the habit of inspecting your own behavior before looking for the other contributing factors to a problem. Ask for feedback from others. Collaborate to improve the community, starting with improving yourself. Be humble, be aware, and always be learning.

How to Exit a Community

For whatever reason—good, bad, or indifferent—sometimes you need to withdraw from a project and its community. How do you do that? You may be surprised to learn that the reason doesn't actually matter and has no impact on the steps you should take to be a good free and open source citizen as you leave the community. These steps are similar to the ones you would take if you were to leave a job, so they shouldn't seem unfamiliar.

- *Commit or submit all of your work in progress.* If you've already started working on an issue or feature and have made some progress on it, make sure to submit those changes to the project so others can build upon your work rather than having to start all over again.

- *Leave all issues you're working on in a good state.* "Good state" here means that it will be easy for someone else to pick up where you left off. This will require you to restate the problem you're working on, summarize the progress you've made so far, list what remains to be done, and include a pointer for where people can locate your work in progress.

- *Transfer knowledge.* If you haven't done so already, update (or add) the documentation with the knowledge and information that you gained during your time with the project. Without this step, everything you learned will be lost to the community when you leave.

- *Transition access to resources.* Do you have access to certain resources, such as servers or administrative access to repositories? Make sure that this access is transitioned so it's not lost when you leave. This also can help ensure the security of the project. After all, when someone is holding the keys to the kingdom, you don't want them to fall into the wrong hands.

- *Communicate expectations.* If you don't let people know that you're leaving, they may expect that you'll still be available to answer questions or help out with development. Drop a quick line to the mailing list (or whatever communication channel makes sense), letting people know that you're leaving, that you won't be contributing anymore, and how to contact you should they have questions. There's no requirement to go into details about why you're leaving.

- *Leave all communication channels and repositories.* Simply unsubscribe from these things.

That's all it takes. You've now withdrawn from the community. Of course, depending on what you've been working on, this process could take a while to complete, so don't try to rush it. Regardless of your reason for leaving the project and community, it's always a good idea to be respectful as you withdraw. Even if you've had a bad experience in the community, don't get angry and figuratively flip a lot of tables as you storm out. That's not a good look for anyone. Take the high road and leave calmly and quietly. Related to that and to a point I made above: There is no requirement that you must tell the community why you are leaving. A simple, matter-of-fact, "As of this date, I will no longer be contributing" is perfectly fine. If the reason you're leaving is that the community was unwelcoming, unhelpful, or rude, you may feel tempted to provide feedback about that on your way out the door. Before you do so, ask yourself: Would a community that treated you like that care about your feedback? Would it make any difference? Odds are the answer to both of these questions is, "no," so save yourself the time and just walk away from the toxic environment, with your dignity intact.

You Don't Have to Feel Trapped

All through this chapter I've emphasized that you have the power to get out of a bad situation. I honestly cannot say this often enough: You do *not* need to have a thick skin to contribute to free and open source software. You do *not* need to tolerate demeaning or rude communities. You do *not* have to invest your time in a project where the community does not respect you. You *do* have the power to change your situation. As you come across problems when contributing to a FOSS project, either the problems detailed here or others, consider the return on your investment to overcome them. Consider whether it's actually worth your time to do so. Consider whether you might not have other options for projects. And then, if you find that the investment will not have a good return, withdraw from the project. If the project is unresponsive or does not appreciate your contribution, withdraw from the project. If the community tolerates assholes and assholery, withdraw from the project. There are millions of free and open source software projects out there. Leave the unhealthy ones behind you and seek out projects where you and your contribution are respected, or if you prefer, you can always start a project and a community of your own. This can be very fulfilling, but is easier said than done. The next chapter gives you tips for how to launch your own project and make it successful.

CHAPTER 10

Start Your Own Project

Contributing to someone else's project is all well and good, but what about starting your own? While you could just whip up a project and throw it out on a code forge somewhere, you'll get a lot better results if you pay attention to the small but important details that make a project worth using and worth contributing to in the first place.

This chapter assumes you want to release a personal project. Releasing a project for work may share a lot of the same steps, but it's a different matter entirely and is covered in the next chapter. Company-released projects often differ in scope, but they always differ in risk tolerance, intellectual property considerations, and strategic reasons for releasing the project. These characteristics make a very large difference in how you approach releasing a FOSS project, and messing them up can result in enormous costs.

Which is to say: This chapter is for your own personal use. If you would like to release a project for your company, seek professional (FOSS, not psychiatric) help. Your first stop should be Karl Fogel's excellent book, *Producing Open Source Software*.[1] Whereas the book you're reading tells you all about how to contribute to a project, Karl's does a masterful job of telling you how to release one, especially (but far from exclusively) how to release one from within a company.

Quick Start Guide to Releasing Your Own Project

I strongly encourage you to read and follow all of the tips in this chapter, but if you're in a big rush and simply must get your project out the door immediately, there's a very short list of non-negotiable files you must include to ensure projects of any size can be successful:

---

1.   https://producingoss.com

- A README file
- A user guide
- A CONTRIBUTING file
- A Code of Conduct (CoC)
- A license, properly applied

"A Code of Conduct? Really?" I hear you asking, and I answer, "Yes, really." Codes of Conduct didn't used to be required for free and open source project success, but now they're table stakes; it's just something you include, because your project looks archaic without it. Many people will not participate in or contribute to a project if it doesn't have a Code of Conduct, and this mindset is growing as more people start contributing to FOSS. A CoC is quickly becoming one of the bare minimum things needed for your project to gain adoption and contributors. Don't shortchange your project's potential by not including one.

The other three items on the list—a license, a user guide, and a CONTRIBUTING file—are obviously required. Without a license file, it's illegal for anyone to use (or perhaps contribute to) your project without speaking with you. Without a user guide, it's very difficult for anyone to gain value from using your project. Without a CONTRIBUTING file, no one knows how to submit a contribution to the project.

Overall, these four files tell the story, "I share my project with you under these free and open conditions. Here's how you can use it to get things done. If you find a problem or want a new feature, here's how you can help. You are welcome here and can feel safe in this community." That's a very compelling story and more likely to attract both users and contributors. If attracting those is appealing to you, make sure your project has these four things at a bare minimum. However, if the bare minimum isn't good enough for your project and you'd like to do things the *right* way rather than simply *right away*, read on.

What Is Your Goal?

You want to release your project as free and open source...but why? It seems like it's a silly question with an obvious answer, but is it, really? When you pause to consider it, you may find that it's not quite as easy to answer as you first expected, but that answer can be very useful when considering the steps that follow. Your goal may be to share the project, but otherwise to minimize your involvement with it (what we call the "throw it over the wall" method). This is common with very small projects like utility libraries that your company doesn't use often anymore but others may find useful later on. Perhaps you're looking for help with development, so you need to build a community of users and contributors. Projects that can be of use across an industry but don't expose any proprietary information can be useful to release in this way, allowing competitors to become collaborators on non-differentiating functionality. Are you releasing it because it's the right thing to do? Projects developed using public funding should be accessible to the public who paid for them, for instance.

Knowing the answer to the question, "What is my goal?" can help you focus your efforts as you prepare the project for release. If all you want to do is "throw it over the wall" and get it out there, you may be able to get away with investing a bit less time and effort in the release preparations. If, instead, you need to attract and keep users and contributors, then you know already that you'll need to spend a lot more time on documentation and procedures before you release the project to the world. Releasing a well-documented project is like saying, "Who wants cookies?" at a daycare: it gets attention and makes you the most popular person in an otherwise crowded room. Just don't assume that you know why you're releasing it or what will be required to do so. Pour a nice cup of tea and take a few minutes to think it through before starting work on releasing that project of yours.

Optimize for Community

Unless you are just throwing your project over the wall, you probably want to attract users and contributors to it, which is to say: you want to build a community. There are entire organizations[2,3] dedicated to helping people learn how to build communities, so I won't cover it in detail here. However, if you've gotten this far into the book, you already know a lot of the elements that can help lead to a strong and effective community. Optimizing your new project for these elements can put you on the right path toward attracting users, contributors, and collaborators.

The elements necessary to optimize for community are also those that help to establish, build, and maintain the trust of other people. It's important when implementing these elements that you remain entirely authentic and open. If you dissemble in any way, even if you think you're very clever about it, people will know, and they will rescind any trust they had given to you and your project. Once that trust is lost, it's difficult bordering on impossible to regain. It also undermines the project's chances of having a good reputation,

---

2. https://communityroundtable.com
3. https://www.feverbee.com

meaning you're less likely to attract new community members. Step carefully when establishing these elements to make sure you're not at risk of that sort of unpleasantness.

So what are these elements that can help establish, build, and maintain trust while simultaneously building community? You know them already:

- An enforced Code of Conduct: Having a Code of Conduct in your project shows people that you care about their comfort, safety, and well-being, as well as for the overall health of the project. It's a sign that the community is here to improve the project and that unprofessional or rude behavior, which would sabotage that effort, is not welcome. People know that they can make their contribution and join the community without fear of personal and unwarranted attacks based upon attributes such as gender, sexual orientation, religion, or age among others.

- A CONTRIBUTING guide: A CONTRIBUTING guide is a sign that the project community understands and has anticipated the needs and difficulties of new contributors. The guide may have bugs when first launched, but that's to be expected. Doing your best to put yourself in the mindset of a new contributor, understanding their perspective, and trying to provide the information they need shows potential contributors that you care about and respect their time.

- Abundant documentation: This entire book is about contributing and contributors, but they're not the only ones who require documentation. Most often someone is a user of the project before they become a contributor; however, if the user documentation is nearly non-existent, then no one will enjoy using the project and you'll have lost a large pool of potential contributors. Do your best to provide a guide for how to install, use, and troubleshoot the project. If the project has an API, document that with all parameters and return values and provide sample code. If you make it easy for someone to use your project, you'll be making it easy for them to join the community as well.

- A responsive community: Users, contributors, and community members all have the same limited time availability as you. It can be quite frustrating to have a personal project put on hold because you're waiting to hear back on a question or a contribution to a FOSS project. Respect the time of others and try to build a community culture of quick communication. That communication doesn't have to be a detailed answer or review of a contribution, but it should at least acknowledge receipt of the question or contribution, express gratitude for it, and set up an expectation for when the sender can hope to receive a more detailed response...and then follow through on that promise. Minimizing the times when your project or community becomes a bottleneck for others helps to establish a very good reputation.

All of these tips really come down to one thing: *Have empathy for others.* Put yourself in their shoes and try to anticipate questions, problems, or needs they may have. This empathy creates a culture and environment that's attractive to new users and contributors and can lead to building a community more quickly than you anticipated. It also becomes a lead-by-example sort of situation. As new community members see you being empathetic and understanding to new users, new contributors, and new community members, they themselves are likely to emulate this behavior and be empathetic and understanding themselves. Empathy becomes, simply, "the way we do things around here," and generates a positive cycle of welcoming new members to your community.

Work in the Open

Before releasing your project, you may have worked on it in secret or just for your own purposes. Perhaps you enlisted the help of some folks, but in general you worked behind closed doors and outside of the potentially critical gaze of onlookers. That all changes the moment you release it; from there on out it will be free, open, and public. All of the development processes around it should similarly be free, open, and public; otherwise you will lose the trust of your users and contributors both.

These processes are not limited to the mechanical "create contribution-review contribution-merge contribution" development steps, though they're certainly important to perform openly and in the public eye. The processes also include the product management and roadmap of the project. You may be used to guiding the project in whatever direction makes the most sense for you and your purposes, but once you release it and have users, that guiding must shift to what makes the most sense for the community. While a few large project communities are able to get away with having a Benevolent Dictator for Life, even they don't unilaterally impose their will upon the direction of the project features and instead consider the overall good to the project and the community.

Releasing a project implies to the community that you're open to collaborations of all sorts. They will expect to have input into the direction of the project and the ability to shape that direction through their contributions. If you're not willing or do not have the time to collaborate or accept contributions from community members, I encourage you to rethink your decision to release the project as free or open source.

Keep It Simple, Silly

We in the software world love to get mired down in the details. We'll spend hours thinking and arguing about the minutiae, whether we need to or not. Add to that a tendency toward perfectionism and you have a recipe for what's called *premature optimization*, or trying to optimize a program or process before you've had the chance to see whether that optimization is even needed. When premature optimization occurs while trying to prepare a project to release as FOSS, there's a very good chance that the release will be delayed indefinitely as everything is over-considered, over-architected, but undoubtedly under-documented.

If you've never released a FOSS project before, you naturally want to do everything possible to make sure it goes smoothly. You want every single bug to be fixed. You want all of the code to be pristine. While that's admirable, it does open the door to that premature optimization. Instead of focusing only on the code, work to keep the entire process and all policies you establish for the project very simple and as clear as possible. Use the time you would have spent on premature optimization to make sure that the project and its policies are well documented. The combination of a simpler, easier to follow process and clear documentation about it not only encourages people to use and contribute to your project, but it also saves you time from having to answer relatively simple questions.

Starting out with simple processes and policies doesn't preclude adding complexity later, should you find it necessary. In fact, you'll find that your simplicity will scale and allow for modifications much more easily than any complexity you would have implemented earlier on. This allows for a lot of flexibility should the project community grow beyond just a few contributors. Having simple processes also imposes less mental burden on you and the project community members, who don't have to work through decision trees just to decide whether to approve a contribution.

There's a time and a place for complexity, to be sure, but that time is not right at the launch of your project into the FOSS world. Keep it Simple. You'll be glad you did.

Share the Burden Early

It's becoming more common now to hear stories of FOSS maintainers burning out and walking away from their projects. This isn't a new phenomenon; for as long as there have been free and open source projects, maintainers have been burning out on them. What's new is that people are recognizing that burnout is bad, that they don't have to put up with it, and that if they share their stories, they may help inspire others not to burn out like they did.

Now—as you prepare to release your project—is a good time to start thinking about how to prevent or minimize your own burnout as its maintainer. Much of the advice in this chapter will help with that, as it will reduce some of the burden you'll have in answering questions of users and new contributors. Setting up your own boundaries is also very helpful, as is sharing what those boundaries are. For instance, if you can only spare a few hours every other weekend, include that information in the CONTRIBUTING file to set up expectations for when they might hear from you.

While documentation, boundaries, and other types of expectation setting will go a long way toward avoiding burnout, nothing makes as large of a difference as having other people to help you. By sharing the burden of project maintenance, you reduce the impact on any one person while improving the project's *bus factor* and therefore, also its longevity and resilience. As early as possible, look for contributors who communicate well, provide quality contributions, participate in discussions, and are generally engaged with the community. Then ask these people whether they would like to become a co-maintainer of the project. You'll naturally have to sort out exactly what "co-maintenance" looks like for your particular project, in collaboration with your new partner. This may take a few conversations or email threads to get right, but once you've all figured out the details, make sure to document them in the project. This sharing of the collaboration and the role that each maintainer plays in the project is part of what makes FOSS such a powerful movement and development philosophy. Open is better.

Select Communication Routes

If one of your goals for releasing the project as FOSS is to start building a community of users and contributors around it, you'll need to communicate with those people. How do you do that? What's the best communication route for a FOSS project?

The glib but true answer is, "The best communication route is the one that the community will use." You're just starting out here, though. How do you know which communication route your community will use? How can you make it easy for them to participate and join the community when you don't even know what the easiest way is for them to do that?

You could do real user and market research here, reaching out to potential project users and contributors and asking them for their communication route preferences. Yes, you surely could do that, or you could recognize that any decision you make at this time is just going to change once the project reaches a certain level of community involvement anyway, so you may as well just start with whatever (reasonable) communication method is easiest for you. After all, for a while at least you're likely to be the one and only community member on this thing. While considering your user and community members' needs is never wasted time, you also have to consider your own. Maintaining a FOSS project takes a lot of time, so until you have help with that, anything you can do to make the task a little less onerous on you is a good move.

Prefer email? Set up a mailing list. Prefer that all communication go through the issue tracker? OK! No problem! Do you want people to contact you through a real-time chat system before opening an issue? Great, good to know. Whatever communication routes and methods you prefer, document those and share with the nascent community the expectations you have around communication. It's perfectly OK for you to have a preference, as long as you express it and make it easy for people to accomplish their goals while still meeting your communication expectations.

Whatever communication routes you prefer, keep in mind that if you select a route that's easy to locate and use, then people are much more likely to...well...to locate and use it. While I do encourage you to discover your own personal preferences as to communication route, I also encourage you to balance that with the needs of your potential users and contributors. You are always free to embrace your personal communication route preference of encrypted messages shuttled by specially trained beagles, but if you do so, you're also free not to be surprised when no one bothers to communicate with you or to use the project.

What About Issue Tracking?

It's a very rare FOSS project that doesn't use an issue tracker of some sort. Yours is unlikely to be an exception to that rule, so if an issue tracker is in play...how do you want people to use it? Sure, you may think you don't care, but that not-caring will last only until someone submits an issue that doesn't at all adhere to your previously latent and unexpressed preferences for how to write a good issue.

Before you release your project, take a few minutes to consider what you would like to see in an issue, and then, to document those guidelines as well as guidelines for the care and feeding of an issue. Walk people through the stages an issue passes through on the way toward completion and/or closure. If necessary, set up issue tags or statuses to help reflect where an issue is in its life cycle. Tags such as awaiting review, duplicate, and in development (among others) not only show people where an issue is in its life cycle, but they also help reduce the number of questions you receive as people wonder what's going on with the issue they reported.

Some hosted version control systems like GitHub and GitLab support defining templates that display whenever someone starts reporting a new issue. These templates can be very helpful for gathering the information you'll need to reproduce the problem. For instance, if the platform or operating system is a factor that can influence the performance of the project, you can set up an issue template to request these bits of information. A template isn't required, but you may find that setting up a basic one will help improve the quality of issues you receive for your new project.

Whatever life cycle you choose for the issues in your project, I encourage you to keep it as simple as possible. Like I said before, simple is easy to understand as well as being easy to change. Don't get stuck in the premature optimization trap by setting up a complicated Enterprise Grade Issue Workflow for a small FOSS project. Making it difficult for people to report and work on issues means you've also made it less likely that anyone would want to in the first place. Do have and document your process preferences, but try not to go overboard. Keep it lightweight for now and then add complexity later (and only if it's actually necessary).

Styleguides

While you should definitely keep things as simple as possible at launch time, styleguides are one piece of complexity you may wish to add. You may not have thought about it very much yet, but I suspect you have some pretty strong opinions on how code, documentation, design, usability, accessibility, or other elements of a project should be done. If you don't tell people about these preferences up front before they start to contribute, you'll likely find that the first contribution you receive will be in a style that grates on your nerves like fingernails on a chalkboard. Why subject yourself to that—and the contributor to having to re-style their contribution—if you can avoid it by writing up a simple styleguide or two?

The key word there is, of course, *simple*. A styleguide doesn't have to be anything involved, and frankly it's more likely to be read and followed if it's not. A list of preferences contained in a file named coding_styleguide.md or documentation_styleguide.md can be easy to create, maintain, and use. For instance:

```
# Coding Styleguide

* Spaces not tabs
* 4-space indents
* Start and end curly brackets on own lines, not indented
* Use trailing commas
* Use semicolons

Not sure how to style something? Create an issue with your question.
```

There are standardized styleguides that you can use if you'd rather not maintain one of your own. For instance, Google provides styleguides for a large number of programming languages[4]. These are available under a Creative Commons Attribution license and therefore free to use, modify, and redistribute as long as you provide attribution to Google for the original work. These styleguides are commonly used in software development teams around the world, so you and your potential contributors may already be familiar with them. Some of these styleguides are formatted such that they can be imported or used by an Integrated Development Environment (IDE) or a continuous integration system, ensuring that the style is applied before someone merges a non-compliant contribution into the project.

Whatever styleguide you decide to use—your own or one provided by another group—make sure you enforce it. Rules that aren't enforced aren't rules; they're just noise and they add unnecessary cognitive burden on everyone who encounters them. If you don't have the time or inclination to enforce styleguides, don't include any when you launch your FOSS project. But if you have even a few preferences, you may want to document them in a very simple styleguide like the previous example.

Select a License

For most of this chapter you've probably been thinking, "We're really concerned about licensing. When is she going to talk about licensing? Because this is free and open source software, and we know that means we need to talk about licensing." The answer to that is, "Now, at the end of the chapter, because

---

4. https://github.com/google/styleguide

it's the last thing you should do before releasing the project." The license used for the project may be influenced by the license on the component parts (for instance if the project relies on something released under a copyleft or reciprocal license), or it may be influenced by business needs. There are many things you need to consider before selecting a license, and all of those things were covered earlier in this chapter. Only now, once you've completed those steps, are you ready to start considering which license to apply to the project before you release it.

Whether I'm speaking with new contributors, people interested in releasing their projects, or companies engaging with FOSS for the first time, the same questions come up over and over again: "Which free/open source license is best? Which should I choose?" The answer to each of these questions—which if you've gotten this far into the book, should not surprise you in the least—is, "It Depends."

Objectively speaking, there is no "best" free and open source software license. Compared against each other, devoid of any other context, there's no way to rank them. They simply exist, and have no meaning or significance until they're compared with a person's or project's needs, beliefs, and preferences. Once placed against such a backdrop, it can become much easier to see whether a particular license is a good fit for what the project wishes to accomplish.

Which is to say: before you choose a license, determine what you wish to allow or constrain people to do with your project. That's what licenses do: define the conditions under which the project may be used by others. So…what conditions do you wish to impose? Do you want to require anyone who uses your project, should they distribute their own project, to do so under the same terms as yours? Do you believe that people should share and share alike, reciprocally? Do you want to encourage others to support the Four Freedoms and for your software to be free forever? Then you want to use a copyleft license like GPLv3[5]. Alternatively, do you just not care at all and just want to get the project out there under whatever license? Do you not care what people do with the project after you release it, just as long as you receive credit for it? Then you want the MIT[6] or 3-Clause BSD[7] licenses. If your project is writing, art, or a similar creative work, then you'll want to use a Creative

---

5.   https://www.gnu.org/licenses/gpl-3.0.en.html

6.   https://opensource.org/licenses/MIT

7.   https://opensource.org/licenses/BSD-3-Clause

Commons[8] license instead. The Open Source Initiative maintains a list[9] of the most popularly used licenses, which can serve as a helpful starting point.

If you remember from *The Foundations and Philosophies of Free and Open Source*, there's an entire spectrum of free and open source licenses, spanning from very reciprocal to very permissive and everything in between. It's worth taking the time to think through license selection to make sure you're choosing one that reflects your beliefs and your preferences for how people will use your project. You'll usually find that once you figure out which license fits your personal beliefs, you can use it for all projects you release from there on out, so the selection process may be something you only have to do once.

Myself, I usually prefer to default to the very reciprocal GPLv3 or Creative Commons Attribution-Share Alike licenses. Usually these suit very well for what I'm trying to accomplish, but if I'm working with or for clients or others, then I evaluate those licenses against their particular needs. Sometimes the GPLv3 ends up being the final selection, other times the Apache or MIT licenses are better. There's no real way to tell until you take the time to think things through.

How to Apply a License

Now that you've chosen a license...what do you do with it? You'll be happy to learn that you don't have to do anything Very Official Indeed, such as registering use of the license with any organization. That's not necessary, but applying a license to your project isn't as simple as slapping a LICENSE file into the repository and calling it a day. Remember: the license is a legal document and is tightly intertwined with copyright and intellectual property laws. You didn't really think that anything involving a legal document was actually going to be easy, did you?

OK, that's not fair of me. In fact, while applying a FOSS license to your project may be a little tedious, the process itself is usually quite simple. This is one of the advantages of using an OSI-approved[10] license: a lot of the legal complications are already managed by those reviewing and approving the licenses. All you need to do is select one and do the small amount of work required to apply it properly.

What exactly is the proper application of a FOSS license? You're probably sick of hearing this by now, but: It Depends. Each license has their own

---

8. https://creativecommons.org/choose/
9. https://opensource.org/licenses
10. https://opensource.org/licenses

preferred method for applying it to a project, so you need to do some research to make sure you use the application method that's preferred for your selected license.

While each license varies as to the details of its proper application, the general guidelines are fairly similar for all of them. What follows are those guidelines, but they're just to help you gain familiarity with the basic and bare minimum required for the process. These guidelines also assume applying a license to a brand new project, and they in no way cover changing a project's license, adding a license to an existing and already-licensed project, or any other advanced scenario. For anything like that, seek legal counsel before applying or changing any license. For the basic new-project scenario, use the following guidelines, but again, always research the specific preferences for your selected license.

License File

The first step in applying any license to your project is adding the license file to the repository. This file is typically named LICENSE, LICENSE.TXT, LICENSE.md, or similar, but the GPL family of licenses prefers that this file be named COPYING. Whatever you call it, the file must contain an ASCII or Unicode copy of the exact and complete license text. The only exception to "exact and complete" is that you must modify the file to include your copyright information. For instance, if I were to apply the 3-Clause BSD license to a project I was releasing, I would update the file to include my copyright information as such:

```
Copyright 2018, VM (Vicky) Brasseur
```

```
Redistribution and use in source and binary forms, with or without
modification, are permitted provided that the following conditions
are met:
```

```
1. Redistributions of source code must retain the above copyright
notice, this list of conditions and the following disclaimer.
```

```
2. Redistributions in binary form must reproduce the above copyright
notice, this list of conditions and the following disclaimer in the
documentation and/or other materials provided with the distribution.
```

```
3. Neither the name of the copyright holder nor the names of its
contributors may be used to endorse or promote products derived
from this software without specific prior written permission.
```

```
THIS SOFTWARE IS PROVIDED BY THE COPYRIGHT HOLDERS AND CONTRIBUTORS
"AS IS" AND ANY EXPRESS OR IMPLIED WARRANTIES, INCLUDING, BUT NOT
LIMITED TO, THE IMPLIED WARRANTIES OF MERCHANTABILITY AND FITNESS
FOR A PARTICULAR PURPOSE ARE DISCLAIMED. IN NO EVENT SHALL THE
COPYRIGHT HOLDER OR CONTRIBUTORS BE LIABLE FOR ANY DIRECT, INDIRECT,
INCIDENTAL, SPECIAL, EXEMPLARY, OR CONSEQUENTIAL DAMAGES
```

```
(INCLUDING,BUT NOT LIMITED TO, PROCUREMENT OF SUBSTITUTE GOODS OR
SERVICES;LOSS OF USE, DATA, OR PROFITS; OR BUSINESS INTERRUPTION)
HOWEVERCAUSED AND ON ANY THEORY OF LIABILITY, WHETHER IN CONTRACT,
STRICTLIABILITY, OR TORT (INCLUDING NEGLIGENCE OR OTHERWISE) ARISING
IN ANY WAY OUT OF THE USE OF THIS SOFTWARE, EVEN IF ADVISED OF THE
POSSIBILITY OF SUCH DAMAGE.
```

The only change I made in the license above was the very first line. The remainder of the license file must not be touched. Remember: this is a legal document. If you're not an intellectual property lawyer, don't try changing the document (and even then I'd recommend against it, as the 3-Clause BSD is a well-established license).

Most people know to look for a license file in the repository if they wish to see under which license a project is released, but it never hurts to be helpful in small ways. I recommend adding a quick license and copyright statement to the project's README file to make it that much easier for people to find this information. It doesn't have to be anything nearly as formal and dramatic as the license file above (which is actually quite laid back as licenses go). A simple line or two is all you need:

```
# Licensing

This project is copyright VM (Vicky) Brasseur and licensed under
the 3-Clause BSD license. Please see `LICENSE` for complete
information.
```

Copyright Notice

You have a license file, so you're done, right? Your project is licensed and you can move on to other tasks? Unfortunately, no. Like I said previously, this process isn't as simple as slapping that license file into the repo. The next step is adding the copyright notices.

At a bare minimum, the copyright notice contains the word "Copyright" followed by the name of the copyright holder, the year the work was copyrighted, and a very brief license statement. This notice must be added to every file in the repository.

Yes, really. Every file.

The repository is composed of multiple files, which means that there's a chance those files can and will be separated. If that happens and the copyright notice isn't added to each file, then there's no way for a file's recipient to tell either who to credit for the work or, by virtue of that brief license statement, whether they're legally allowed to use your work at all. Therefore, yes, you must have a copyright statement in each and every file. The task can be tedious, but, well... We're in technology. You can probably figure out how to script this rather than do it manually.

This statement should be placed at the top of every file and be encased in the comment charaters for the appropriate language. Here's an example:

```
<!--
Copyright VM (Vicky) Brasseur, 2018
Licensed under 3-Clause BSD.
Please see LICENSE for more information.
-->
```

Many people complain that a copyright notice takes up a lot of space at the top of the file or otherwise complicates their development workflow, but in all my experience, I've not seen a case of a properly formatted copyright notice causing anything beyond a mild inconvenience, and even that is a rare occurrence. If you find that you notice and dislike seeing the notice in the files, most editors and IDEs have functionality or plugins for "folding" this text so it's both out of sight and out of mind.

Some licenses, such as Apache, recommend that rather than place your own name in the copyright notice, you instead use the text Copyright The Authors, 2018, and then list the project authors in a file named AUTHORS. This can be a very efficient way to handle having multiple people holding copyright over a single project file. This approach works even if you're not using the Apache license, so you may wish to consider it, if you have multiple contributors to the project or expect you will have multiple contributors soon after releasing it.

A Note on Copyright Year

In the United States and other countries that are signatories to the Berne Convention[11], as soon as you create a copyrightable work, you automatically have copyright. In these countries, there's no need to register for copyright or otherwise keep track of it unless you wish to sue to enforce your copyright.

Because there's no need to register for a copyright, there's also no need to track the date for your copyright. It can be handy to have this information, but since most copyrights expire based upon a length of time after the death of the copyright holder, the date of creation doesn't really matter. Despite that, it's best practice to include a date in your copyright statements and notices...but which date should you use and when should you update it?

---

11. https://en.wikipedia.org/wiki/Berne_Convention

The most common advice is to use the year of the most recent "release" of a particular file. Guidance is a bit vague as to what "release" means here. Does pushing a new version of the file to a repository constitute release of the file? Or is it only considered a release when the file is bundled into what we in technology call a "new release" of the entire software package?

To be safe, try this: When a file is first created, use the year that happens in the copyright notice in the file. If the file is updated in a given year, update the year in the copyright notice accordingly. If the file is not updated in a given year, there's no need to update the copyright notice year for that file. This method keeps the copyright notices up to date only when they need to be, and it removes the tedious burden of having to change the year in every copyright notice in every file every year.

Publish the Project and You're Done!

You've written the docs, you've selected and applied a license, you've jumped through the somewhat irritating but necessary hoop of adding a copyright notice to every file. All that remains in the process is to publish the project. Since you're acting on your own behalf here, you'll most likely use a public code forge, such as GitLab, GitHub, or BitBucket. Because each of these have their own specific and well documented steps for publishing a project, I won't cover that here. Simply follow the appropriate steps, publish your project, and stand back to admire your handiwork.

But what if you're not acting on your own behalf? What if you're one of the millions of people who want to contribute to free and open source software projects as a part of your job? That's a different matter entirely, and the next chapter will clear it all up for you.

CHAPTER 11

Contribute for Your Job

Years ago, if you asked your boss whether you could contribute to free and open source software on company time, they would probably have looked at you like you had just sprouted another head. In certain cases—a database or an operating system—you might be allowed to use FOSS in your job, but it was highly unlikely anyone would allow you to use company resources to give back to the community. Thankfully those days are starting to be behind us. It's now becoming more common for companies to allow staff to make at least some contributions to the FOSS projects on which their products and services rely, but we're not yet to the point where you can take for granted that your supervisor, team, or company will allow you to contribute while you're on the clock, or even while simply using their hardware and materials.

There are many factors that you need to take into account when you want to start contributing to FOSS as a part of your work duties. You've already learned about some of these factors in earlier chapters, but this chapter expands on those while collecting all of this information in one place for easy reference later on. Also, keep in mind that this chapter is only about *contributing* to FOSS for your job. It's not about *using* FOSS on the job, as that holds a different sort of risk profile for your organization. Before integrating a FOSS project in your company's product, be aware of your company policy as far as compliance, security, and approved licenses. Some companies, for instance, have a blanket ban on using the Affero GNU Public License (AGPL) or other copyleft licenses. Because these FOSS usage policies are highly specific to each company, I do not cover using FOSS for work in this book.

Contributing to External FOSS Projects

Later on I'll briefly talk about how to contribute to FOSS projects released by your company, but the majority of this chapter assumes that what you want to do is contribute to projects that are external to your company. These could be libraries or tools that your company uses as a part of its products or services, or it could be a project that you're fond of for some reason. While the tips are the same for both of these categories, you may find that you have more luck gaining permission to contribute to projects that are somehow important for your company to continue operating. Using company time to contribute to projects that don't impact the company, but that you find interesting, may be a hard sell.

Contributing to external projects can be a risky proposition for your company, thanks to the many complications that fall under the umbrella of Intellectual Property Law. If you receive approval to contribute to these projects, you must be careful not to make any missteps. Doing so can get your company into a lot of legal problems, and that's not a good career move for you. Dot all of your i's, cross all of your t's, and be aware that even small contributions carry a great burden of intellectual property responsibility.

Check Your Employment Agreement

Back in *When It Goes Wrong*, I spent a fair bit of time discussing the complications of contributing to FOSS when you're employed. The short version is that, depending upon your employment agreement, it's possible that your employer owns copyright over all work performed on their equipment, even if that work isn't done on company time. While this can cause obvious problems when you're trying to contribute on your own time, it also complicates contributing for work. That's because a part of contribution, whether it's performed under a CLA or DCO or not, is confirming that you have copyright over your contribution and therefore are allowed to give it to the project. When you contribute for work, it's very possible that your employer owns the copyright over your contribution, and therefore, without their permission, you don't have the legal right to give that work to anyone else.

Remember that copyright ownership grid from *When It Goes Wrong*? If you haven't done so already, get a copy of your employment agreement, read it carefully, and fill in that grid with who owns the copyright to your work in the following situations:

- On company time and company equipment
- On company time but your own equipment
- On your own time but company equipment
- On your own time and your own equipment

Unless you're in the very unlikely position where all of the squares associated with *Company's* show that you own copyright over what you create, you'll need to get permission from your company to contribute their copyrighted work to another party (the FOSS project). When you do contribute that work, unless your company has said in writing that it has assigned the copyright back to you, you must put the company down as the copyright holder of the contribution. The method for doing this varies by situation and project, so make sure you get that straight before you submit your contribution.

Are There Existing Company Policies?

More often these days you'll find that your company has a policy for contributing to FOSS projects. This policy often is based in the software development department, so if you're not already assigned there, you may need to ask someone who is in that department to learn about the policy. Depending on the company, this policy will define what types of contributions you may make, to what types of projects, and under what conditions. For instance, some companies may allow employees to contribute to projects that are on an approved list, while others may allow employees to contribute to any project as long as their contribution is reviewed by an internal committee prior to submitting it to the project. Before you start working on a contribution on company time and equipment, ask your supervisor about the company FOSS contribution policy. It would be a shame to waste hours of your life working on a contribution that you're not allowed to share with the project.

Speaking of your supervisor, even if the company policy allows for contributions to free and open source projects, do check with your supervisor before starting work on that contribution. They're responsible for how you spend your time while on the job, and they may have higher priority tasks for you to work on than fixing a bug on a FOSS project. That may not be something you want to hear, but it's the stark truth about a job: the company is paying you for your time and expertise, so while you're on the job, they get to determine how that time and expertise is applied. It's possible that your supervisor may allow you to spend some of that time on FOSS contributions if you ask, but it's guaranteed they'll be irritated if you spend a lot of company time contributing when they believe there are other tasks that need doing instead.

Confirming company policy is especially important when the project has a CLA or DCO that you need to sign before you're able to contribute. As I mentioned earlier, in a work-for-hire situation, your employer owns the copyright on anything you produce under the conditions specified in your employment agreement, and under those conditions, you cannot legally sign a CLA or a DCO without their permission. Some policies allow for you to sign the CLA or DCO, others allow signing only after legal counsel reviews the CLA, the project, and the contribution, and others don't allow signing at all. It's very important to be clear about these policies before you contribute. While intellectual property laws may not be very important to you personally, they are probably very important to the organization that pays your salary. Don't risk your job simply for a FOSS contribution.

Contributing to Your Company's FOSS Projects

If the company you work for has projects that it's released as FOSS, the steps to contribute to them are obviously going to be very similar to those for contributing to any other free and open source project, with the addition of any internal steps and processes that your company requires.

It can be very tempting, since the project was released by the company you work for, to treat it as though it were simply another work product: you take direction from internal stakeholders, perform the required development, and then release the product to the public. Don't do this. Once a project is released as FOSS, it ceases to be the sole and exclusive domain of the company that released it and now belongs to the community that forms around it. While the company still gets a say in the roadmap of the project, the company is now but one of many stakeholders who must all collaborate to evolve the project in a direction that benefits everyone. The company cannot dictate its will and yet remain a community member in good standing. That sort of behavior is likely to lead community members to fork the project and start a new one where your company has no influence. The company will have lost all the advantages of releasing a FOSS project but will have gained a bad reputation.

Instead, it's very important that the company perform all work on the project in the exact same way that any other community member would. It must use the same tooling, develop on the same roadmap, and work and collaborate in the open. It must engage with the community as equals, not simply as volunteer developers. How this looks in practice will depend on the company, the project, and the community. Sometimes a company releases a project but is unable (or unwilling) to form a community around it or gain any adoption for the project outside of the company itself. In this case the company naturally has no other collaborators and is free to shape the direction of the project as it sees fit. Other times a company releases a project, and it gains a community that includes contributors from competing companies. In this situation, it may make sense for the company to bequeath the project and its copyrights on it to an external non-profit foundation to remove any perception of bias in the governance of the project.

Because of these and many other potential complications, it's often advisable for a company to bring on professional assistance when releasing and managing FOSS projects. Doing so can allow the company to gain all of the benefits of releasing the software while also building and maintaining a healthy community and project ecosystem.

Convincing Your Employer to Support FOSS

The remainder of this chapter addresses how to convince your employer to support free and open source software projects and communities. It's a question that I hear so often that not including it would have been negligent. Note that I say "convince" here, not force, cajole, blackmail, whine, or complain your way to getting your employer to support FOSS. Stamping your little princess foot and demanding the company do something is unlikely to get you the results you want. Instead, you'll need to understand the company's perspective and help the company understand why supporting free and open source software is in its best interests as well as those of the community.

What Type of Support?

While allowing you to contribute to FOSS is one way that the company can provide support, it's far from the only way. Some companies may value your time more highly than other types of investment in FOSS. Consider all of the possibilities, and you may discover forms of support that are helpful to the community while also being palatable to the company. Some of the ways the company can help to support FOSS projects and community are:

- Money: The most obvious and often the easiest form of investment that a company can make in free and open source software is to provide funding. As you know, most projects are developed by volunteers on their own time, so there's not a lot of extra cash lying around to pay for things like meetups and conferences, T-shirts and stickers, bandwidth and hosting, or any of the other incidentals that help to make a project successful. Providing fiscal support to a project community can be a quick and easy process and does not come with the intellectual property risks involved with contributions.

- Contributions: Despite those risks, contributions are still a very good way for a company to support a FOSS project, especially one on which the company relies for its own products and services. Providing documentation, development, design, testing, marketing, or other types of contributions can help the project evolve more quickly than it would without the support.

- Staff: At the most extreme end of the contribution spectrum, a company can dedicate headcount purely for working on the project. This can be especially appealing if the project is a fundamental, core element of the company's product offering. Embedding company staff in the community as dedicated developers can help ensure that vital piece of software and its related community are always healthy and evolving.

Benefits to the Company

No matter how you personally feel about supporting FOSS, your employer is unlikely to make any sort of investment if there isn't something in it for the company. They are, after all, in business, and they have a responsibility to work toward the benefit of the company and its stakeholders. Therefore, before you approach the company about supporting free and open source software, consider the benefit that the company will get out of it. Following are some of the many valuable business benefits from providing this support:

- Word-of-mouth marketing: The holy grail of marketing departments everywhere, word-of-mouth marketing is when people say nice things about the company. The company doesn't have to spend a penny on advertisements or branding efforts, because the customers do all of the talking for them. Of course, this only works if the customers like the company enough to tell their friends about it, so the company has to provide good products, service, and support while also appealing to the customers' own values.

- Recruiting: Supporting the FOSS projects that are used in their products and services is a great way for a company to find and recruit new employees. These candidates are already familiar with the technology the company uses, which can reduce onboarding times and allow the new employees to be productive more quickly than someone who isn't familiar with the project at all.

- Customer support: The company can approach the community with questions if it's having problems using a project. Of course any project user is free to do this for a FOSS project, but as a community member in good standing, the company will be well positioned not only to receive a prompt reply but also to shape any potential fix should one be needed.

- Research and development (R&D): By collaborating on a project on which the company relies, the company (and all other community members) can receive new features and security fixes much more quickly, efficiently, and reliably than if they were to develop those features entirely on their own. The community members become force multipliers for each others' efforts and reduce the time it takes features to get to market.

- Project influence and power: While certainly the least altruistic of these example benefits, there's no denying that supporting a FOSS project and community gives that company influence over the project and potentially power to direct the project as best suits the company's needs. Used wisely, this influence and power can benefit the entire community, not simply the company. Used poorly, the only thing the company will develop is a poor reputation both inside and outside the FOSS community.

These are only a few of the benefits the company could see by supporting free and open source software projects and communities. Obviously not every company will experience every benefit, and not all benefits are valuable to all companies. Which ones are best for your specific employer? That's a question you need to answer before broaching the topic of supporting a FOSS project. The benefits don't have to be anything large or dramatic; they simply have to be commensurate with the investment you would like the company to make in the project and/or valuable enough that the company is willing to make that investment. Take the time to consider which benefits make the most sense for your company's situation.

You'll Need a Plan

Now that you've considered what benefits the company should get from supporting FOSS, it's time to put together your plan for proposing that they do so. Sure, you could just dive right in there and start pestering people, but you're more likely to be successful if you plan first. What you're doing, essentially, is asking a business to make an investment. It's a business deal, and approaching it in a more business-like manner gives your idea a better chance of being accepted. This means you not only need to consider the company's perspective, but you also need to speak their language. If that means PowerPoint and spreadsheets, then PowerPoint and spreadsheets it is, but unless you're planning to propose a very large investment in supporting FOSS, you may not need to go to such lengths. Still, knowing what you're going to say in your pitch and why will make the entire process go more smoothly.

Revisit those benefits you considered above, and list and format them into something more easily understood by your audience of business-focused decision makers. Don't turn it into buzzword bingo. Believe it or not, most business-focused people don't spend all of their time *putting a pin in this so they can circle around to ideate about leveraging the synergistic potentials of this green field opportunity.* They're people just like you, they simply have different priorities in their day-to-day work life than you may. Consider those priorities when formatting the list of benefits and speak directly to them, clearly and succinctly. For instance, if you know that your team will be growing in the next year, rather than saying, "This support will make recruiting easier," say, "This support gives us ready access to a pool of highly qualified candidates already familiar with our technology, making it easier for us to grow the team." Instead of, "It will give us a good reputation in the community," try, "Joining the community helps to build our company reputation among this group of well-connected influencers in our industry." If you're not used to reframing things into this sort of language, don't be afraid to enlist the help of a friend or colleague with more experience in this area.

Benefits are nice and all, but nothing comes for free. As you're creating your FOSS support pitch, you must be very clear about what sort of investment you're asking the company to make, in other words, "What's it gonna cost us?" You may find that some of your audience wants to know the answer to this question first, but if possible, try to prime them for liking the overall idea by leading with the benefits. Once you've done that, briefly detail how much (or little) of an investment is required for the company to see those benefits. This could be a statement as simple as, "If we sponsor this FOSS conference for $2000, we get our logo on the website and on all the banners at the event, plus we get a five-minute talk during the keynotes before an audience of 500 developers." Or it could be as complex as a budget broken down by expenditure per month. Be sure to list all of the potential costs, and recognize that they may not all be monetary. In-kind contributions (for instance, donating the company's products and services) and staff time are all part of the investment package and shouldn't be overlooked.

The final part of your plan is the implementation details. List the very specific steps, timings, milestones, and deliverables for the investment, as well as who is responsible for making them happen and metrics to determine that everything is still on track. It's possible that a small investment won't have very much happening for implementation. The conference sponsorship, for example, may not require a lot of coordination or activity beyond wiring money, sending a logo, delivering a short talk. Alternatively, it could include a brand awareness study before and after the event to see whether the investment changed brand perception at all; it all depends on what the company needs to justify whatever investment you're suggesting they make or to prove that they're receiving the expected benefits. Having implementation details considered in advance shows your audience that you've thought things through and are not just asking them to make an investment without any real idea of how to pull off your crazy scheme to support a FOSS project. It helps to reassure them that their investment is more likely to pay dividends for the company as well as the community.

Play the Long Game

Depending upon your goals for convincing your employer to support FOSS projects and communities, it may make sense to start with a very small plan. Small plans are easier to implement, easier to prove they worked, and can prove that you know what you're talking about. Altogether, these characteristics create small successes that can lead to larger forms of support later on. Just as importantly, should the small plan fail, it's unlikely to cause much ill-will in the company. Small investments that provide little to no measurable benefit are much easier to dismiss than a large investment that flops. For instance, if your long-term goal is to have the company release some of its critical utilities as FOSS projects, it may make sense to start by developing the process to contribute bug or documentation fixes to a library or utility that the company uses in its products or services. This not only has the effect of easing the company into contributing to FOSS, but it also lays the groundwork for the processes and policies that will be required for the company to release its own projects.

It's very tempting to dive right in with an ambitious plan to have the company support a community with development time, in-kind donations, and event sponsorship, but it's much more difficult to pull off a plan like that, and it requires a considerably larger investment in company resources than allowing people to submit bug fixes to a critical project. When an ambitious plan fails, it typically fails dramatically and in a way that discourages further investment in free and open source projects and communities. So even if your Grand Plan involves several types of investment and involvement, break it up into smaller bits and start with just one of them to give the plan the best chance of success.

Small or large, any plan takes time to see through to the end. Even with the relatively simple example of having the company sponsor a small FOSS community conference, it can take several months from proposing the plan to seeing any sort of results. For more ambitious plans, it can take even longer. As you're creating your plan, take this long time frame into consideration and build it into the implementation milestones. This will set up the expectation that, however worthwhile, it will take some time for the company to see a return on its investment. Setting up that expectation up front can minimize the pressure to deliver results immediately.

Check with Lawyer and Accountant

Depending upon the type of investment you wish your employer to make in FOSS, it may make sense to check with the company's lawyer and accountant during the plan-making process. It's smarter to do this up front rather than being surprised by legal or regulatory problems after receiving approval. This may not be possible, if these roles aren't held by people who have full-time jobs at the company. Some companies have a lawyer and accountant on retainer, but you may not have access to them. That's OK. There's no requirement to check with them in advance. If you think that their advice will be helpful, it may suffice to note that in your plan, if only to let people know that you're considering all of the possibilities.

Some situations where consulting a lawyer may be wise include anything having to do with company intellectual property, including FOSS contributions created on company time or equipment. If the support you have in mind includes an in-kind donation of company services or products, it can be helpful to confirm that the company is not taking on a potential liability or risk with the donation. For instance, if the company donates storage and hosting to the FOSS project and then the project gets hacked and all of the private data stored in the company's service is stolen, will the company be held liable? It's good to make sure you know the answers to questions like this before starting any company FOSS support program.

Accountants come into play whenever money enters the picture, but in particular, they are very helpful for understanding the potential tax implications of any support the company provides to a FOSS project. Some of these projects are members of registered non-profit foundations or are registered non-profits in their own right. The company's support may therefore be tax deductible, which would be an extra benefit. On the other side of the coin, there are some situations where the company may take on a tax burden with their support. Were the company to pay a salary to a core project contributor and that person is not based in the same locale as the company, depending on the location of the contributor, it may create a new *tax nexus* for the company. That would be an unfortunate surprise, so you may want to check with a friend on the company's finance team before finalizing your FOSS support plan.

It's not always necessary to consult a lawyer or an accountant when creating your plan, but the simple examples above show how valuable it can be to do a little due diligence before proposing that the company commit itself to a potentially risky FOSS support program.

Potential Pitfalls

You may convince your employer to start supporting FOSS projects and communities in some way, but it's still possible that things won't work the way you expected. As a matter of fact, the entire plan could fail, taking the company's investment in FOSS with it. Aside from the obvious reasons for avoiding this, a side-effect of this failure can be that the company withdraws from any sort of FOSS support. They may continue to use it, but having been burned, they won't again risk making an investment in free and open source software communities.

These failures don't occur in a vacuum, and usually you can see them coming a mile away if only you know to look and prepare for them. Some of the most common reasons for failure in a corporate FOSS support effort are:

- Lack of preparation: There's a cliché that says, "if you fail to prepare, prepare to fail." It's cheesy and doesn't even belong on inspirational posters, but it's still a true sentiment. The majority of FOSS support efforts that I've seen fail have been caused by people diving in without appropriate knowledge of the community or the goals for company involvement. Spending an afternoon thinking these things through can go a long way toward ensuring success in the support effort.

- Lack of metrics: You've asked the company to invest in supporting a FOSS project or community, but how can you tell whether the company is actually getting anything out of it? While good intentions can get you pretty far in this effort, if you're not able to show a return on the company's investment, then this FOSS support project will be low-hanging fruit when budget cuts come along.

- Wrong or over abundant metrics: If there's one thing we're good at in technology, it's collecting data. If there's one thing we're bad at in technology, it's using data. As you start the FOSS support project, make sure you know what the company wants out of it. Without this information, it's impossible to find the relevant signal in the noise that is all the possible data that could come in from the effort.

- Not allowing enough time: All too often, a company will start supporting a FOSS project or community only to withdraw that support in a few months because they haven't yet seen a return on their investment. These companies haven't been primed to understand how much time it can take to receive the benefits of supporting a free and open source project or community, so they are understandably disappointed. Doing a better job of setting up expectations about delivery of those benefits, as well as being open and clear about the milestones of the support effort, can help prevent that disappointment.

Obviously, these aren't the only ways a FOSS support effort can fail, but they are some of the most common. The point isn't to list all of the various permutations of failure that might beset your planned corporate FOSS support effort, but to make you aware of some of the possible roadblocks you might face. If you're serious about this effort, pay some attention to how the process might trip on its path and try to clear those roadblocks before you get there (or at least to route around them). A little foresight really will go a long way.

While the benefits for your company will be a lot different from the benefits to you as an individual contributor, they're no less real. Despite the potential risks, if you take the time to think through the benefits and plan the implementation of a company FOSS support effort, it can lead to a win-win situation for company and community alike.

Forge Your Future

And now here you are, some 180 or so pages later, at the end of a long journey toward learning how to contribute to free and open source software projects. You may not yet know all there is to know about contributing, but you've successfully learned more than enough to get started and be an effective contributor and community member. You probably started this book thinking that it was going to be very technical and were surprised when it was not, but by now you've learned that while technical knowledge and skills are usually necessary to contribute to FOSS, human knowledge and skills are much more important for success.

These human skills of empathy and communication are not only more important than the technical skills, they're also more difficult to master. However, you'll find that while the required technical skills will vary from project to project, these human skills will apply to all projects equally. Master these and you'll find you're not only able to be a great FOSS contributor, you'll also excel in your job, hobbies, or any other undertaking that requires interaction between people. In this way, contributing to FOSS truly does help you forge your future.

Glossary

While many of the terms below can have multiple meanings, the definitions provided all assume the context of free and open source software projects, communities, and contributions.

accessibility

The process of opening up access to the software to as many people as possible. This could mean making sure the color scheme is good for people who are color blind, confirming that the software is usable by a screen reader, providing text alternatives to audio content, and other potential actions that can enable more people to use the project.

ad hominem

A Latin phrase meaning, "to the person," ad hominem statements are those that address qualities of the person at the receiving end rather than the qualities of someone's contributions. For instance, saying, "You're dumb for thinking that" is addressing the person and can rightfully be seen as a personal attack. "That is not a good idea" addresses the concept being discussed rather than the person who proposed it. Avoid ad hominem statements whenever communicating in FOSS projects and communities.

API

Short for *Application Programming Interface*. An API is the external "face" of a piece of software. It details how to communicate with the software programmatically and allows different software packages to connect and interact.

atomic commits

A version control commit that addresses a single (usually small) topic, fix, or feature. Atomic commits are considered safer than large, unwieldy commits. The relatively small size and scope allow an atomic commit to be reviewed more easily and thoroughly and is easier to roll back should something go wrong. Both the review and the easy rollback mitigate the risk of fatal bugs slipping into the project.

BDFL

Short for *Benevolent Dictator For Life*. BDFLs are rare in FOSS but they do exist. For example, Guido van Rossum was the BDFL of Python and Dries Buytaert is the BDFL of Drupal. A BDFL is typically the founder of the project. They have final say in and can veto all decisions related to the project, but it's very rare that they use this power. Typically a BDFL will lean on the *Benevolent* part of the title by seeking consensus and always working toward what's best for both the project and its community.

birds of a feather

Also known as *BoF* or *Open Space*. A BoF is an informal gathering of people interested in a similar topic. Many FOSS conferences and events provide BoF meeting space to give communities a way to gather, meet each other, and discuss matters related to their specific topic.

branch

In a version control system, a branch is simply a pointer to a specific commit in a repository, creating a new path for work on the repository. Working on a branch allows you to isolate development from other parts of the repository, so you can work without risk of affecting unrelated features or code.

breakout session

Often called simply *sessions*, these are scheduled training events at FOSS conferences. Each breakout session features one or more presenters who deliver information to the audience. Sometimes a session will be a panel of people answering questions posed by a moderator.

bug

Something that doesn't look or act right in a system. Typically bugs are found in software, but the term is also applied to things like human interactions, FOSS governance, or other facets of FOSS development.

build

Refers either to the process of creating a distributable version of the FOSS project or the distributable version itself. The build process will be different for most projects. It may require compiling code, running a test suite, or other steps. Causing an error in the build process is called "breaking the build."

bus factor

A number equal to the number of team members who, if run over by a bus, would put the project in jeopardy. The worst possible bus factor for a project (or part of a project) is *one*. If only one person is familiar with that piece of the project, and that person goes away for some reason, the project will find itself in a very uncomfortable position.

CI/CD

Short for *Continuous Integration/Continuous Deployment (or Delivery)*. In a CI/CD process, merging a commit into a repository automatically starts running the entire test suite. If all tests pass, then the repository (including the newly merged change) are automatically deployed to either a test or production system.

clone

A standalone copy of a repository, or alternatively, the process of copying a repository.

commit

The process of submitting a change to a version control system, or alternatively, another name of the change itself.

commit bit

Having a *commit bit* means that someone is allowed to merge changes into the project version control repository. There is no physical thing (*bit*) involved. It's simply a phrase that originates in the access control systems of legacy version control systems, where a commit access was controlled by the value of a single binary digit (a bit). Those bits are gone, but the *commit bit* term remains.

commit message

Text describing what's changed and/or fixed in a commit to a version control system. The commit message should be as detailed as necessary and include not only what was changed but also why. If the work in the commit is associated with an issue, the issue number should also be included in the commit message.

community

A self-organized and self-identified collection of people sharing a concern or interest. Many FOSS projects have communities associated with them.

continuous deployment

The *CD* in *CI/CD*. See the entry for CI/CD for more information.

continuous integration

The *CI* in *CI/CD*. See the entry for CI/CD for more information.

contribution

Documentation, testing, design, programming, event coordination, or any other action that helps a FOSS project.

Contributor License Agreement

Also known as *CLA*. This is a legal document intended to certify that the person sharing a contribution has the right to do so, and that once the contribution is accepted, the project has a license to alter, distribute, and administer those contributions however it sees fit. Once in a while the CLA will also transfer copyright for the contribution from the contributor to the project or the project's organizing body. The intention of a CLA is to minimize potential legal complications of distributing the work.

copyleft

See the entry for reciprocal license.

copyright

The right given to the creator of a work to decide how and under what conditions that work may be used by other people and organizations. In most countries the creator automatically receives copyright over a work as soon as it's created, but in countries that have not signed the Berne Convention, the creator may be required to apply for copyright over their work.

core contributor

Someone with extensive knowledge and experience in the FOSS project. Core contributors usually hold some sort of leadership position in the project, if only informally. They often are responsible for maintaining the quality of the project and guide the project's development roadmap.

design pattern

An accepted best practice for solving a certain type of software design problem. A design pattern is a very general description of how the problem is best solved. The generality of the description makes it applicable across different programming languages and applications.

Developer Certificate of Origin

Also known as *DCO*. A confirmation by a developer that they have the right to share their contribution with the project. The developer provides their confirmation by "signing" their contribution using a -s flag on the git commit. The DCO is intended as a paperwork-free and low hassle alternative to the CLA. Because it requires use of git to sign a commit, the DCO can only be used by projects that use the git version control system and on contributions that are tracked in version control.

diff

Either a specially formatted output showing the differences between two files (or two versions of the same file), the process of creating the output, or a utility that creates the output. Often used in conversations about a contribution, such as "Did you diff this before commiting it?" and "Check the diff and you'll see it's just whitespace changes."

domain knowledge

Specialized knowledge about a certain topic, industry, or area of interest (*domain*). People outside of the domain are unlikely to be familiar with this knowledge. For instance, a knitter has domain knowledge about how to read a knitting pattern, the different types of needles available, and the different types of fibres used in yarns, among other related information. Domain knowledge is important when making judgement calls about the design and implementation of a project for a domain. People who have relevant domain knowledge are known as *subject matter experts*.

DRY

Short for *Don't Repeat Yourself*. DRY is a best practice in software development. Any time you find yourself in a situation where you might need to reuse a piece of code, design element, or other component, DRY encourages you to pull it out into its own reusable fragment (function, method, file, or whatever makes sense). In this way, if a change is needed, it only needs to be made in a single place rather than in a series of repeated components. This reduces the chance of introducing bugs.

employment agreement

Sometimes called an *employment contract* or simply *contract*. This is the thing you sign or otherwise agree to when you start working for a person or organization. The employment agreement defines details like how much you'll be paid, whether you get vacation time, and—most importantly in the context of a FOSS contribution—who owns the copyright over what you create while on the job or while using the employer's equipment.

environment

In a FOSS context, *environment* doesn't refer to trees, oceans, and the like. It refers to the combination of software and hardware where a FOSS project runs. If you're developing the FOSS project, you may have a *developer environment* composed of your laptop, a local installation of the software, and your IDE or text editor. Once you're done developing, you may install the project in a *testing environment* running on a single server in the cloud with limited network ability and a sample database. After testing is complete, you may install the project in a *production environment*, running on a large collection of cloud-based servers that are accessed by many people and both reads from and writes to a large database.

feature branch

Also known as a *topic branch*. Simply a branch in the version control system, created, used, and destroyed as you would any other branch. What makes a feature branch a feature branch is that you've created it specifically so you can work on a single feature. Once the feature is complete and merged into the main branch of the version control system, you can delete the feature branch.

forge

Also known as *code forge*. A web-based service for hosting the source files for FOSS projects. A forge will usually provide features like access control, version control, and an issue tracker. Some forges will also provide online editing for the source files, a wiki, CI/CD services, and other features related to software development. GitLab, GitHub, and BitBucket are three popular forges.

fork

For such a short little word, *fork* carries an awful lot of baggage and responsibility in FOSS. The original and primary meaning of the word in this context is to take a copy of an existing project, rename it, and start a new project and community around the copy. It could also be used as a verb for that entire process. While this kind of fork requires some technical work (version control, renaming, things like that), it is primarily a social action. Despite this existing use of the term in FOSS, in 2008 GitHub decided to use the word *fork* to represent the action of a git clone command, instead of using the word clone. The word *fork* has now come to mean both copying a project to start a whole new project and community, as well as copying (cloning) a project simply to inspect or work on it.

FOSS

Short for *Free and Open Source Software*. Sometimes you'll see the same concept abbreviated *F/LOSS* for *Free/Libre and Open Source Software*, *OSS* for *Open Source Software*, or *OS* for *Open Source*. This book uses the abbreviation *FOSS*.

"Free as in..."

Spend any time in FOSS and you'll very soon see statements that start with these three words. The three most common variations are "Free as in Speech," "Free as in Beer," and "Free as in Puppy." The *speech* and *beer* variations are from a quote by Richard M. Stallman and are related and play on the multiple meanings of *free* in the English language. "Free as in Speech" uses *free* in its *libre* sense: few restrictions placed on the thing. "Free as in Beer" uses *free* in its *gratis* sense: no monetary cost. "Free as in Puppy" also plays on the *gratis* meaning of *free*, but with the added complication that comes from bringing a living, breathing thing into your life. The meaning here is that even if you pay nothing for the software (or puppy), you are on the hook for its maintenance and welfare. So while there is no up-front cost, there is an ongoing one.

free software

Software that provides the Four Freedoms. For supporters of free software, just as all people should be free from slavery, oppression, and abuse, all software should be free from any restrictions of inspection, use, reuse, and distribution. For them, software freedom is a moral matter. Nearly all free software is also open source software.

governance

The way that a FOSS project and its community are run and operated. This can include the roles in the project (core contributor, contributor, user), how decisions are made and communicated, whether there are elections for certain roles and if so how to perform those actions, among other social and political structures necessary for keeping the project and its community running smoothly.

hallway track

All of the learning that occurs outside of scheduled sessions (that is, in the hallway) of a FOSS community conference or meetup. Many people find the hallway track to be the most valuable part of any conference.

IDE

Short for *Integrated Development Environment*. A usually complicated piece of software used to develop other software. Most IDEs include a text editor, a diff tool, and a debugger along with related software development tools. Visual Studio and Xcode are two popular IDEs.

infosec

Short for *information security*. The practice of maintaining the privacy and security of data and systems, including preventing unauthorized access to them, securely deleting data when it's no longer needed, and being careful with what data and access is necessary in the first place.

inline reply

When replying to an email, embedding your replies in the body of the original message, immediately below the piece to which you're responding, and optionally deleting the parts of the original message you're not addressing in your response. Some FOSS communities prefer that people use inline replies to mailing list messages.

integration test

Tests to determine whether the individual parts of a system will still work as expected when you integrate them together. For instance, if you were running a basic integration test on a car, the wheels may each roll well individually, but when you attach them to the chassis and test again, you learn that the wheel wells are too small and the wheels no longer turn.

intellectual property

Anything that's the result of you using your mind (*intellect*). Writing, drawings, technical inventions, music, and other creative works are a few of the things that qualify as intellectual property. There's a large body of law dealing with intellectual property. It covers things like patents, trademarks, and copyright. Because the work that goes into creating FOSS is copyrightable, intellectual property is a pretty big deal in free and open source software.

interface

An interface is how a person or system interacts with a piece of software. This could be a user interface (UI), a graphical user interface (GUI), a command line interface (CLI), or an application programming interface (API). Interfaces are important to get right, as having a difficult interface of any sort means it's less likely someone will want to use the software.

IRC

Acronym for *Internet Relay Chat*, a real-time chat system invented in 1988 and commonly used in FOSS projects and communities. While IRC is a popular avenue for communication in FOSS, it's only one of many different real-time chat options.

issue

Also known as *ticket*. A general term for all of the bug reports, feature requests, and support questions related to a FOSS project.

issue tracking

> The process of maintaining and monitoring a collection of issues. Issue tracking typically includes ways to comment on, tag, flag, or close/resolve issues. Nearly every FOSS project will use some sort of issue tracking and many forges include issue tracking functionality.

license

> Also spelled *licence*. A legal document declaring the conditions under which a piece of intellectual property may be used. Licenses are the backbone of FOSS. Without an OSI-approved license, a FOSS project is not considered "open source". Without a license at all, it's illegal for anyone to use a software project, as doing so violates intellectual property laws.

linting

> Static analysis of code (without needing to run it) to find common or potential errors. There are automatic linting tools for most programming languages. Linting often occurs as a part of the testing process. Sometimes a FOSS project will have a linter set up as a part of the CI/CD system, so each commit to the repository will be linted before it's merged.

listserv

> Another name for a mailing list. The original mailing list software—which is still under active development today, but no longer used as frequently by FOSS projects—is named *LISTSERV* (all caps, yes). The name of this software became a general term often used for all mailing lists.

lurking

> Joining a real-time chat room, mailing list, or other communication avenue used by a FOSS project, but only listening to the conversations rather than participating in them. Lurking is a good way to get a sense of the community around a FOSS project: how they interact, who the key players are, and whether they're welcoming to new contributors.

mailing list

> An email group on a specific subject. Most FOSS projects use a mailing list (also known as a *listserv*) of some variety as one of its communication routes, and some FOSS projects prefer the listserv to other forms of communication.

meetup

> A typically informal gathering of people. FOSS communities can be globally distributed, making it difficult to gather and collaborate. Frequently, instead of a large global gathering, community members who live near each other get together at meetups to discuss the FOSS project and get

to know each other. Sometimes the meetups can be quite large, but usually they're no larger than a couple dozen people (and often much smaller than that).

merge request

> See the entry for *pull request*.

open source software

> Software that is released under a license that has been reviewed by the Open Source Intiative and certified as providing all the freedoms of open source as detailed in the Open Source Definition. Software released under a license that is not approved by OSI by definition cannot be "open source" software, since it is not guaranteed to provide the freedoms defined in the Open Source Definition.

Pac-Man Rule

> When standing or sitting around in a circle having a conversation, leave a gap in the circle. This gap—which if viewed from above would make the circle resemble the Pac-Man video game character—provides an opportunity for others to join in the conversation. The Pac-Man Rule is an effective way to strengthen a community by creating a space that's more inclusive of people who may otherwise lack the confidence to step into a closed circle.

pastebin

> A web-based service for pasting then sharing large blocks of plain text. Pastebins help to keep emails, issues, and real-time chats more readable. Rather than, for instance, pasting a long log file into an email, you can paste that log into a pastebin then share a link to it in the email. It's best practice in FOSS communities to use a pastebin to share plain text that's more than a few lines long.

patch

> See the entry for *pull request*. This may also refer to the *patch* utility, which is used for creating a *patchfile* that can be submitted as a contribution to a FOSS project.

permissive license

> A type of open source license that states that someone who makes a change and redistributes the software is *permitted* to change the terms and conditions under which someone can use the new distribution (also known as a *derivative work*). In other words, derivative work can be released under a different license from the original work, even if that

license is proprietary. The Apache License and MIT License are two popular permissive open source licenses.

ping

Mentioning someone in a real-time chat system. So called because some real-time chat clients notify the person of the mention with a sound or a visible change to the client. Sometimes used as a verb for generally reaching out to someone: "I'm going to ping Ioana about the high load on the production server."

platform

The environment that runs a piece of software. Platform can include operating system, browser, chipset, and other relevant components of the system. Which components are relevant depend on the software being run. For instance, for a web-based Javascript application, the user's browser, browser version, and operating system may be the only relevant components, whereas for compiled software, chip architecture and operating system may be the most relevant components of the platform.

premature optimization

Spending a lot of time and effort to "improve" something before you know whether or what type of improvements are needed. Premature optimizations can devour a lot of valuable time and are considered a worst practice in software development.

Principle of Least Astonishment

A convention in software and system design which says that if a design has the chance to surprise people with an unexpected interface or result, then that design should be thrown out in favor of one that will not surprise anyone. While it's usually applied to software development and user interface design, the Principle of Least Astonishment works in all situations where people might be caught off guard. For instance, if you would like to institute a new rule or policy in a community, discuss it and its reasons first, rather than simply popping it on people.

project

A collection of software and the people, policies, and procedures that come together to build and maintain that software. If the software is released under an OSI-approved license, then this collection is called an *open source project*.

proprietary license

A software license that is not approved by the Open Source Initiative. Most proprietary licenses are created by companies and organizations for the software that they sell and release as a part of their product or service offerings, and therefore are an important part of the business of software.

pull request

Also known as a *merge request* or a *patch*. A type of contribution to a FOSS project. By submitting the contribution, you are *requesting* that the project *pull* (merge) it into the main repository. Pull requests can be code, documentation, designs, or anything else that is stored in the project's version control system.

real-time chat

An online service that allows people to communicate in real time using text- and image-based messaging. Most FOSS communities use some sort of real-time chat system as one of their communication routes. IRC, Mattermost, Telegram, Discourse, and Rocket.chat are some popular real-time chat options used by FOSS communities.

reciprocal license

Also known as *copyleft license*. The conditions of a reciprocal license ensure that a work released under one can never be released under a license that may in any way remove or diminish any of the original rights and freedoms granted to the user by the license. A redistributed or derivative work released under a reciprocal license must also not add new restrictions to what the user may do with the work. This ensures that the work, once freed, will forever be free. Reciprocal licenses also have a requirement that if a work licensed under one of them is included in a derivative work that is then redistributed, that derivative work must be released under the same terms and conditions as the reciprocally-licensed work. That is the *reciprocal* nature of this type of license: if your creation benefits from a reciprocally licensed work, then anyone who receives your creation must similarly benefit. The GNU General Public License (GPL) is the most common reciprocal license. Some others are the GNU Lesser General Public License (LGPL) and the Mozilla Public License (MPL).

repository

Often abbreviated as *repo*. A version-controlled collection of code, documentation, images, and any other files necessary for the operation of the FOSS project. Repos usually have a single, central source. Each copy (*clone*) of that central source is also called a *repo*, but may be called a *local repo* to distinguish it from the central source.

roadmap

An ordered plan for the development of a FOSS project. A roadmap usually includes a list of features and bug fixes, loosely organized into a release schedule. Having a roadmap allows the FOSS project to plan the resources and time required for development, while also allowing it to establish feature delivery expectation for the users of the project.

RTFM

Short for *Read The F'ing Manual*. The meaning of the *F* in this acronym is left as an exercise for the reader. The acronym is often used in FOSS project communication as a not-so-gentle reminder to people that they should read the documentation prior to asking questions. While it can get the attention desired, using RTFM in conversation is often rude and unhelpful. It's far more effective to send a link to the appropriate documentation.

scope creep

When a feature or bug fix starts with a small set of requirements, but over time accumulates more and more requirements, greatly increasing the scope (and therefore also the risk as well as the time to complete) for the feature or bug fix. Scope creep is an anti-pattern in software development and should be avoided by any means possible.

scrollback

In real-time chat systems, the conversation that occurred while you were away from the chat session. Some systems store this for you automatically, while others (such as IRC) require a special setup to store and view scrollback.

significant whitespace

In programming languages, whitespace (space and tab characters) that has semantic and syntactic meaning in the code. This means that if you get the whitespace wrong, the program will not work (or not work as you expect). Python is the most popular programming language that uses significant whitespace. Some others are Haskell and YAML.

source control

See the entry for *version control*.

squash

Taking a series of version controlled commits and condensing (*squashing*) them into a single commit. Some FOSS projects require a commit squash before you submit your contribution.

subject matter expert

Also known as SME. See the entry for *domain knowledge* for more information.

test suite

A collection of unit, integration, and other tests run against software to ensure that it does what is expected (and does it in the right way). Running a test suite is typically an important step in CI/CD.

ticket

See the entry for *issue*.

top posting

When replying to an email, placing your replies at the top of the message and leaving the original message untouched below it. Some FOSS communities prefer that people use top posting when replying to mailing list messages.

topic branch

See the entry for *feature branch*.

triage

Reviewing an issue to confirm you understand the problem, can duplicate it, and it isn't already fixed elsewhere. Doing issue triage takes time up front, but it saves time during the implementation of the fix for the issue. While some FOSS projects prefer that more experienced contributors triage issues, others are thrilled to have less experienced people lend a hand as the first responders to any new issues that arrive.

unconference

A "conference" where the session schedule is emergent and defined by the attendees, who also provide the material for each session. The entire conference therefore is driven by its participants. The freeform schedule of an unconference allows a FOSS community to discuss topics that are most relevant to them at that very moment, unlike a regular conference schedule that may be determined months in advance.

unit test

A test of one discrete piece of a software system. The *unit* being tested should be the smallest reasonable piece of the overall piece of software, for instance a method or function.

upstream

The primary repository for a FOSS project. All clones of that repository are considered to be *downstream*. It's best practice to push changes to downstream repositories back *upstream*, sharing them as contributions to the FOSS project.

UX

Short for *User eXperience*. Every interaction that a person has with a FOSS project and its community contributes to that *user's experience* with the project. Optimizing for a positive UX is the best way to increase a project's user base and therefore also its community.

version control

Also known as *version control system*, *source control*, and *VCS*. Processes and tools for tracking and maintaining a collection of files as they are modified. Version control can be used for source code, configuration files, documentation, design artifacts, or any other digital file. Version controlled files can be edited by multiple people—sometimes even simultaneously—and then all of the edits can be merged into a canonical version of the file. At the time of writing, git is the most popular version control system for free and open source software projects. Examples of other VCSs are Subversion, Mercurial, Perforce, and CVS.

whitespace

Space and tab characters. For some programming languages, the amount of whitespace in the code can make a big difference to how the software operates. See the entry for *significant whitespace* for more information.

word of mouth marketing

Marketing outreach that's encouraged by a person or organization but is implemented independently by individuals sharing their own opinions. Also known as, "telling your friends and colleagues about things that you like." Word-of-mouth marketing is very effective for building a positive brand; many companies participate in and support FOSS projects and communities to gain a good reputation among the community members who may then tell their friends about just how great the company is for providing its support.

WSL

Short for *Windows Subsystem for Linux*. A method for running Linux utilities and programs on the Microsoft Windows operating system. WSL is a critical tool for people who wish to contribute to FOSS projects but who do not have access to a computer that runs Linux or macOS, since most FOSS projects assume that their contributors are not running Windows and do not optimize their contribution processes for it.

Bibliography

[BBFV01] Roy F. Baumeister, Ellen Bratslavsky, Catrin Finkenauer, and Kathleen D. Vohs. Bad Is Stronger Than Good. *Review of General Psychology.* 323- 370, 2001.

[Del17] Laura Delizonna. High-Performing Teams Need Psychological Safety. Here's How to Create It. *Harvard Business Review.* https://hbr.org/2017/08/high-performing-teams-need-psychological-safety-heres-how-to-create-it, 2017.

[Sca07] Walt Scacchi. Role Migration and Advancement Processes in OSSD Projects: A Comparative Case Study. *29th International Conference on Software Engineering (ICSE'07).* 2007.

[YK03] Y. Ye and K. Kishida. Towards an Understanding of the Motivation of Open Source Software Developers. *25th International Confererence on Software Engineering (ICSE'03).* 419-429, 2003.

Index

Thank you!

How did you enjoy this book? Please let us know. Take a moment to email us at support@pragprog.com with your feedback. Tell us your story and you could win free ebooks. Please use the subject line "Book Feedback."

Ready for your next great Pragmatic Bookshelf book? Come on over to https://pragprog.com and use the coupon code BUYANOTHER2018 to save 30% on your next ebook.

Void where prohibited, restricted, or otherwise unwelcome. Do not use ebooks near water. If rash persists, see a doctor. Doesn't apply to *The Pragmatic Programmer* ebook because it's older than the Pragmatic Bookshelf itself. Side effects may include increased knowledge and skill, increased marketability, and deep satisfaction. Increase dosage regularly.

And thank you for your continued support,

Andy Hunt, Publisher

Level Up

From daily programming to architecture and design, level up your skills starting today.

Exercises for Programmers

When you write software, you need to be at the top of your game. Great programmers practice to keep their skills sharp. Get sharp and stay sharp with more than fifty practice exercises rooted in real-world scenarios. If you're a new programmer, these challenges will help you learn what you need to break into the field, and if you're a seasoned pro, you can use these exercises to learn that hot new language for your next gig.

Brian P. Hogan
(118 pages) ISBN: 9781680501223. $24
https://pragprog.com/book/bhwb

A Common-Sense Guide to Data Structures and Algorithms

If you last saw algorithms in a university course or at a job interview, you're missing out on what they can do for your code. Learn different sorting and searching techniques, and when to use each. Find out how to use recursion effectively. Discover structures for specialized applications, such as trees and graphs. Use Big O notation to decide which algorithms are best for your production environment. Beginners will learn how to use these techniques from the start, and experienced developers will rediscover approaches they may have forgotten.

Jay Wengrow
(220 pages) ISBN: 9781680502442. $45.95
https://pragprog.com/book/jwdsal

Better by Design

From architecture and design to deployment in the harsh realities of the real world, make your software better by design.

Design It!

Don't engineer by coincidence—design it like you mean it! Grounded by fundamentals and filled with practical design methods, this is the perfect introduction to software architecture for programmers who are ready to grow their design skills. Ask the right stakeholders the right questions, explore design options, share your design decisions, and facilitate collaborative workshops that are fast, effective, and fun. Become a better programmer, leader, and designer. Use your new skills to lead your team in implementing software with the right capabilities—and develop awesome software!

Michael Keeling
(358 pages) ISBN: 9781680502091. $41.95
https://pragprog.com/book/mkdsa

Release It! Second Edition

A single dramatic software failure can cost a company millions of dollars—but can be avoided with simple changes to design and architecture. This new edition of the best-selling industry standard shows you how to create systems that run longer, with fewer failures, and recover better when bad things happen. New coverage includes DevOps, microservices, and cloud-native architecture. Stability antipatterns have grown to include systemic problems in large-scale systems. This is a must-have pragmatic guide to engineering for production systems.

Michael Nygard
(376 pages) ISBN: 9781680502398. $47.95
https://pragprog.com/book/mnee2

Pragmatic Programming

We'll show you how to be more pragmatic and effective, for new code and old.

Your Code as a Crime Scene

Jack the Ripper and legacy codebases have more in common than you'd think. Inspired by forensic psychology methods, this book teaches you strategies to predict the future of your codebase, assess refactoring direction, and understand how your team influences the design. With its unique blend of forensic psychology and code analysis, this book arms you with the strategies you need, no matter what programming language you use.

Adam Tornhill
(218 pages) ISBN: 9781680500387. $36
https://pragprog.com/book/atcrime

The Nature of Software Development

You need to get value from your software project. You need it "free, now, and perfect." We can't get you there, but we can help you get to "cheaper, sooner, and better." This book leads you from the desire for value down to the specific activities that help good Agile projects deliver better software sooner, and at a lower cost. Using simple sketches and a few words, the author invites you to follow his path of learning and understanding from a half century of software development and from his engagement with Agile methods from their very beginning.

Ron Jeffries
(176 pages) ISBN: 9781941222379. $24
https://pragprog.com/book/rjnsd

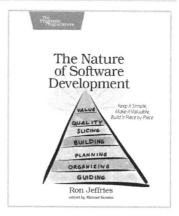

The Joy of Mazes and Math

Rediscover the joy and fascinating weirdness of mazes and pure mathematics.

Mazes for Programmers

A book on mazes? Seriously?

Yes!

Not because you spend your day creating mazes, or because you particularly like solving mazes.

But because it's fun. Remember when programming used to be fun? This book takes you back to those days when you were starting to program, and you wanted to make your code do things, draw things, and solve puzzles. It's fun because it lets you explore and grow your code, and reminds you how it feels to just think.

Sometimes it feels like you live your life in a maze of twisty little passages, all alike. Now you can code your way out.

Jamis Buck
(286 pages) ISBN: 9781680500554. $38
https://pragprog.com/book/jbmaze

Good Math

Mathematics is beautiful—and it can be fun and exciting as well as practical. *Good Math* is your guide to some of the most intriguing topics from two thousand years of mathematics: from Egyptian fractions to Turing machines; from the real meaning of numbers to proof trees, group symmetry, and mechanical computation. If you've ever wondered what lay beyond the proofs you struggled to complete in high school geometry, or what limits the capabilities of the computer on your desk, this is the book for you.

Mark C. Chu-Carroll
(282 pages) ISBN: 9781937785338. $34
https://pragprog.com/book/mcmath

The Pragmatic Bookshelf

The Pragmatic Bookshelf features books written by developers for developers. The titles continue the well-known Pragmatic Programmer style and continue to garner awards and rave reviews. As development gets more and more difficult, the Pragmatic Programmers will be there with more titles and products to help you stay on top of your game.

Visit Us Online

This Book's Home Page
https://pragprog.com/book/vbopens
Source code from this book, errata, and other resources. Come give us feedback, too!

Keep Up to Date
https://pragprog.com
Join our announcement mailing list (low volume) or follow us on twitter @pragprog for new titles, sales, coupons, hot tips, and more.

New and Noteworthy
https://pragprog.com/news
Check out the latest pragmatic developments, new titles and other offerings.

Save on the eBook

Save on the eBook versions of this title. Owning the paper version of this book entitles you to purchase the electronic versions at a terrific discount.

PDFs are great for carrying around on your laptop—they are hyperlinked, have color, and are fully searchable. Most titles are also available for the iPhone and iPod touch, Amazon Kindle, and other popular e-book readers.

Buy now at *https://pragprog.com/coupon*

Contact Us

Online Orders:	*https://pragprog.com/catalog*
Customer Service:	*support@pragprog.com*
International Rights:	*translations@pragprog.com*
Academic Use:	*academic@pragprog.com*
Write for Us:	*http://write-for-us.pragprog.com*
Or Call:	+1 800-699-7764